WARFARE Prayers FOR WOMEN

**BOOKS BY QUIN SHERRER
AND RUTHANNE GARLOCK**

The Beginner's Guide to Receiving the Holy Spirit
God Be with Us
Grandma, I Need Your Prayers
Lord, I Need to Pray with Power
Lord, I Need Your Healing Power
Praying Prodigals Home
The Spiritual Warrior's Prayer Guide
A Woman's Guide to Spiritual Warfare

BY QUIN SHERRER

Hope for a Widow's Heart
A Mother's Guide to Praying for Your Children

**BY RUTHANNE GARLOCK
(WITH H. B. GARLOCK)**

Before We Kill and Eat You:
Tales of Faith in the Face of Certain Death

WARFARE *Prayers* FOR WOMEN

Securing God's Victory in Your Life

**QUIN SHERRER AND
RUTHANNE GARLOCK**

a division of Baker Publishing Group
Minneapolis, Minnesota

© 1998, 2020 by Quin Sherrer and Ruthanne Garlock

Published by Chosen Books
11400 Hampshire Avenue South
Bloomington, Minnesota 55438
www.chosenbooks.com

Chosen Books is a division of
Baker Publishing Group, Grand Rapids, Michigan

Printed in China

All rights reserved. No part of this publication may be reproduced, stored in a retrieval system, or transmitted in any form or by any means—for example, electronic, photocopy, recording—without the prior written permission of the publisher. The only exception is brief quotations in printed reviews.

ISBN 978-0-8007-9970-0

Library of Congress Cataloging-in-Publication Control Number: 2019950850

Portions of this book previously published in 1998 by Vine Books / Servant Publications under the title *Prayers Women Pray*.

Cover design by Rob Williams, InsideOutCreativeArts

Copyright information continued on page 264.

20 21 22 23 24 25 26   7 6 5 4 3 2 1

We gratefully dedicate this book to the
women who have impacted us . . .

In Our Prayer Life:
Freda Lindsay
Elizabeth Alves
Cindy Jacobs
Dee Eastman
Mary McLeod
Cindy Finberg
Eleanor Workman

In Our Writing Journey:
Ann Spangler
Kim Bangs
Jane Campbell
Jane Hansen Hoyt
Elizabeth Sherrill

Prayer is a powerful thing, for God has bound and tied Himself thereto. None can believe how powerful prayer is, and what it is able to effect, but those who have learned it by experience.

—*Martin Luther*

Contents

Introduction 15

Part 1 Praying with Power

I Am God's Daughter 20
The Power of Agreement 22
Speak, Lord; I'm Listening 24
Come, Holy Spirit 26
Praying with Persistence 28
Fasting with Prayer 30
Praise as a Weapon 32
Seeing the Invisible 34
Declaration 36

Part 2 Praying against Hindrances

Letting Go of Unforgiveness 38
Avoiding Deception 40
Overcoming Anger 42
Victory over Fear 44

Saying No to Worry 46
Judging Others 48
No Complaining! 50
Yielding to Temptation 52
Defeating Selfishness 54
Resisting God's Guidance 56
Sin Patterns That Harass 58
Conquering Shame 60
Balancing Priorities 62
Declaration 64

Part 3 Praying for Life's Milestones

Graduation 66
Engagement 68
The Wedding 70
My Firstborn 72
A Brand-New Year 74
Moving Again 76
Making Our House a Home 78
My Nest Is Empty 80
Mother-in-Law Prayer 82
Now I'm a Grandmother 84
Christmas Remembrances 86
Easter Celebration 88
Declaration 90

Part 4   Praying for Children and Grandchildren

Lord, Give Us Children!   92

For the Child in My Womb   94

For Health and Protection   96

For My Special-Needs Child   98

For My Newly Adopted Child   100

My Child Is Sick   102

For My Stepchildren   104

For My Wayward Child   106

Education and Career Choices   108

For Increase and Favor   110

For My Children's Future Mates   112

For My Adult Children   114

For My Grandchildren   116

Declaration   118

Part 5   Praying for Family and Friends

Prayer for Unsaved Loved Ones   120

Prayer for My Husband   122

For My Husband's Career   124

For My Husband's Challenging Job   126

For My Unsaved Husband   128

Prayer to Strengthen Our Marriage   130

For Estranged Family Members   132

For My Friends   134

Prayer to Mend Broken Relationships   136
Prayer to Bless My Parents   138
Forgiving My Parents   140
For My Aging Parent   142
For a Parent with Dementia   144
Overall Daily Prayer for Family   146
Declaration   148

Part 6   Praying When Single
Thank You for My Friends   150
It's Not Easy Being Single   152
Reaching Out to Others   154
Thank You for My Family   156
After a Broken Relationship   158
A New Relationship   160
Single after a Divorce   162
Single Again as a Widow   164
Declaration   166

Part 7   Praying through Tough Times
Dealing with Trauma   168
Help Me Get through the Day   170
Falsely Accused   172
Overcoming Disappointment   174
Lord, I Need Finances   176

Lord, I Need a Job   178
Lord, I Need Healing   180
Trading Self-Pity for Hope   182
Death of a Loved One   184
Declaration   186

Part 8   Praying in My Senior Years

My Senior Years   188
Lord, I'm Lonely!   190
Help Me Make New Friends   192
Here Am I; Use Me   194
I Need Legal Help   196
Praying When a Shut-In   198
Hope for Widows   200
Leaving a Legacy of Prayer   202
My Remembrances   204
Fight the Good Fight   206
Praising God in My Golden Years   208
Declaration   210

Part 9   Praying for My Community and Nation

Prayer for My Pastor and Church   212
Corporate Prayer for My Country   214
For My Neighborhood   216
For Our Schools   218

Prayer for My Community   220
Prayer for the Unborn   222
For Regional Disasters   224
For Our Nation's Defenders   226
Lord, Protect Our Nation   228
For My State   230
Prayer for Elections   232
Prayer for Our President   234
Wisdom for Government Leaders   236
For the Judicial System   238
Prayer for the Media   240
For the Entertainment Industry   242
Declaration   244

Part 10   Important Prayer Helps
A Most Important Prayer   246
The Lord's Prayer   248
Worship Starters   250

Part 11   Scriptures for Intercession and Warfare
Understanding the Enemy   254
God's Answers and Promises   258

Introduction

"Me, find time to pray? When? How? Why?"

As you hurry through your busy, nonstop days, perhaps you have thought, *No way can I carve out time or find the words to express what I want to pray*. Hold on. This book was written with you in mind. Consider your lifestyle, situations and challenges for a moment, and realize that God, your Creator, wants to communicate with you. "Give us . . . daily," Jesus taught His disciples to pray. Since prayer is our vital link to God, this book offers golden "time bites" that will help you strengthen that link.

More important than the *form* of your prayer is the *fact* of your praying frequently to keep the divine connection viable. Prayer is simply talking to God as you would talk to your best friend. Express your deepest feelings. Admit your mistakes. Ask for His help. Listen for His answers—an essential element in effective prayer!

But are you aware that you have an adversary, an archenemy named Satan, God's enemy and yours, who tries to wreak havoc in your life? His tactic, and that of the demonic forces colluding with him, is to stir up strife and division, disrupting family relationships. The goal is to overwhelm you with fear, anxiety, anger, doubt, guilt, insecurity. Giving in to these emotions can hold you back from exercising your God-given authority to resist such attacks.

When we intercede, we stand in the gap—meaning we stand between God and the people or situations we are praying about. In spiritual warfare we battle the enemy to break his assignment, using the weapons God has provided for us: the Word of God, the name and power of Jesus, the blood of Jesus, worship and praise, and fasting. Of course, Christ's victory over Satan is complete and irreversible. Yet we have a role in enforcing that victory.

Whether we like it or not, a spiritual war is going on around us, and godly women have a special interest in this battle. It all began when Satan deceived Eve in the Garden and God put enmity between woman and the serpent. God declared that her seed—Jesus—would fatally bruise the head of the serpent (see Genesis 3:15 AMP).

Since we live in a culture that is increasingly hostile to biblical values, we can equip ourselves to stand firm against these demonic attacks. Scripture gives instruction for spiritual warfare, along with many assurances of victory if we persist in pushing back the enemy.[1]

---

1. Our book *A Woman's Guide to Spiritual Warfare* (Chosen, 2017) is an excellent instruction manual for prayer warriors seeking victory over the enemy.

You can transform your spiritual climate and begin to perceive your circumstances differently by using the weapons of warfare that God provides. We have found that praying prayers of agreement with one or more women prayer partners is also a powerful weapon. Keep in mind that every spiritual battle you fight will strengthen and prepare you for battles you will face in the future. Since there is power in the spoken word, it would also be helpful for you to speak aloud the declaration you will find at the end of each section of prayers.

Please note that in numerous instances in this book, we alternate between using masculine and feminine pronouns in prayers for family members or other individuals. As you pray these prayers, you can change the wording so that it applies to your circumstances. Also note that in part 9, "Praying for My Community and Nation," the first nine prayers are written as global prayers applicable to most countries in the world. The last seven prayers, beginning with "For My State," are written primarily with our country, the United States, in mind. Throughout that section, however, you can adapt the language to suit your specific country.

This compilation of intercessory and warfare prayers, plus declarations and an arsenal of Scriptures, will help you pray with power. Today, you can experience a more effective prayer life and regain any ground the enemy has taken from you. How? Fight for it! Go to war!

Our hope is that your faith in God and your confidence in His Word will increase as you pray these prayers and decree victory over the adversary.

Now thanks be to God who always leads us in triumph in Christ, and through us diffuses the fragrance of His knowledge in every place.

2 Corinthians 2:14 nkjv

*Quin Sherrer
and Ruthanne Garlock*

PART 1

Praying with POWER

I AM GOD'S DAUGHTER

Good morning, God. This is our new day, and I am Your beloved daughter. I trust You to guide me through Your plans for me today. Keep me within Your boundaries, Your protection, so that I don't go off course. Cause my spiritual eyes to stay alert and my listening ears to be sensitive to hearing Your direction. May I stay aware of Your precious presence in everything I do. Thank You that the Holy Spirit guards against evil spirits interfering with Your purpose for me. Your Word declares that I am more than a conqueror [see Romans 8:31, 37], so I refuse to be intimidated. Thank You that I will have favor, blessings and opportunities as I praise You for another day that I can live to serve You. Help me pray through every obstacle with power. I'm grateful that You are such a loving Father to me, Amen.

For all who are led by the Spirit of God are children of God.

So you have not received a spirit that makes you fearful slaves. Instead, you received God's Spirit when he adopted you as his own children. Now we call him, "Abba, Father." For his Spirit joins with our spirit to affirm that we are God's children.

ROMANS 8:14–16 NLT

And I will ask the Father, and He will give you another Helper (Comforter, Advocate, Intercessor—Counselor, Strengthener, Standby), to be with you forever—the Spirit of Truth. . . .

. . . He will teach you all things.

JOHN 14:16–17, 26 AMP

THE POWER OF AGREEMENT

Dear God, Your Word says that "Two are better than one" [Ecclesiastes 4:9], and I know praying in agreement is a powerful weapon in spiritual warfare. Please guide me to the right friend who will be a faithful prayer partner—one committed to praying with me and for me on a regular basis, whether in person, over the phone or keeping in touch via texting. Lord, as we pray for one another's personal needs and family, may we always remember to keep our prayer requests confidential and hold each other accountable. Also, help me connect with a Spirit-led prayer group—one with a vision to pray for a larger territory, such as the needs of our communities and the nation. Help us be led by the Holy Spirit in agreement with Your will, as we trust You for answers that will bring glory and honor to Your name. Thank You, Lord, Amen.

Again, truly I tell you that if two of you on earth agree about anything they ask for, it will be done for them by my Father in heaven. For where two or three gather in my name, there am I with them.

MATTHEW 18:19–20

Then those who feared the L<small>ORD</small> talked with each other, and the L<small>ORD</small> listened and heard. A scroll of remembrance was written in his presence concerning those who feared the L<small>ORD</small> and honored his name.

MALACHI 3:16

SPEAK, LORD; I'M LISTENING

*L*ord, I desire to hear Your voice and be led by You. I know that when You speak to me through my thoughts, Your direction will be consistent with Your Word and Your character. You convict, while the enemy condemns. Your voice leads, while Satan drives. So in Jesus' name, I command evil spirits to be silent. Lord, if the Holy Spirit is speaking, please cause the thoughts I have as a result to become more urgent, and make it clear if and when You want me to take action. Thank You, Father, for speaking to me by whatever means You choose—a Scripture, a dream or pictures in my mind, through someone's words, a song, a strong witness in my innermost being, or even a miracle. Renew my mind to grasp a better revelation of Your Word, and sensitize me to receive thoughts inspired by You. Speak, Lord, and then help me hear and obey, Amen.

For nothing is secret that will not be revealed, nor anything hidden that will not be known and come to light. Therefore take heed how you hear.

Luke 8:17–18 NKJV

Likewise the Spirit also helps in our weaknesses. For we do not know what we should pray for as we ought, but the Spirit Himself makes intercession for us with groanings which cannot be uttered. Now He who searches the hearts knows what the mind of the Spirit is, because He makes intercession for the saints according to the will of God.

Romans 8:26–27 NKJV

COME, HOLY SPIRIT

Jesus, thank You for the promise to Your followers that after You returned to heaven, You would send another Helper, the Holy Spirit. Thank You that the Spirit drew me to accept You as my Lord and Savior. But I desire to draw closer to You by being fully baptized with the Holy Spirit, to empower me as a more effective witness for You. Holy Spirit, in childlike faith I now invite You to fill me and lead me into a deeper intimacy with You. May I have the boldness to share the Gospel message and to pray unashamedly for and with others, as You lead me. I refuse to listen to the enemy's efforts to intimidate me with accusations that I'm unworthy to receive this promised gift. Holy Spirit, I yield to You now. I'm trusting that Your power, presence and discernment will be with me always, Amen.

He commanded them not to depart from Jerusalem, but to wait for the Promise of the Father, "which," He said, "you have heard from Me; for John truly baptized with water, but you shall be baptized with the Holy Spirit not many days from now. . . . You shall receive power when the Holy Spirit has come upon you; and you shall be witnesses to Me in Jerusalem, and in all Judea and Samaria, and to the end of the earth."

Acts 1:4–5, 8 NKJV

When the day of Pentecost came, they were all together in one place. Suddenly a sound like the blowing of a violent wind came from heaven and filled the whole house where they were sitting. They saw what seemed to be tongues of fire that separated and came to rest on each of them. All of them were filled with the Holy Spirit and began to speak in other tongues as the Spirit enabled them.

Acts 2:1–4

PRAYING WITH PERSISTENCE

Lord Jesus, pray with persistence? Yes, I desire to be more bold, specific and purposeful in intercessory prayer. You commended a man's persistence when he kept on asking, seeking, knocking until a door was opened [see Luke 11:5–10]. Lord, I desire that my steadfast prayers stay focused on Your power, not on trying to convince or persuade You to answer. You are such a loving, caring Shepherd. As an intercessor, I want to be on call to pray for any situation or person You alert me to pray for, until that prayer burden lifts and I feel a release to pray for something else. Make me sensitive to when You are leading me into prayer assignments. May the Holy Spirit help me pray more effectively with bold, continual, relentless prayers that hit the mark and accomplish what is on Your heart. Father, I give You all glory and thanks for every answered prayer, Amen.

For this reason I am telling you, whatever things you ask for in prayer [in accordance with God's will], believe [with confident trust] that you have received them, and they will be given to you.

MARK 11:24 AMP

Pray at all times (on every occasion, in every season) in the Spirit, with all [manner of] prayer and entreaty. To that end keep alert and watch with strong purpose and perseverance, interceding in behalf of all the saints (God's consecrated people).

EPHESIANS 6:18 AMPC

FASTING WITH PRAYER

Lord Jesus, I believe You directed me to fast and pray while I'm seeking direction for the specific situation that's on my heart right now. As I engage in this important element of spiritual warfare, I need Your supernatural strength. Please show me how long I should fast, and show me the most effective way to complete it. I believe fasting will help me become more sensitive to the Holy Spirit's leading for prayer and intercession. It will cause me to see new levels of meaning as I study Your Word. And it will help me more clearly identify the enemy's strategies, so I can stand against his attacks with the spiritual weapons You provide. Lord, I desire to glorify You in this as I follow Your example [see Luke 4] and see victories won for Your Kingdom. May I become more attentive to Your nudge for me to pray with fasting, Amen.

Is not this the kind of fasting I have chosen: to loose the chains of injustice and untie the cords of the yoke, to set the oppressed free and break every yoke?

Isaiah 58:6

Moreover, when you fast, do not be like the hypocrites with a sad countenance. For they disfigure their faces so they may appear to men to be fasting. Truly I say to you, they have their reward. But when you fast, anoint your head and wash your face, so that you will not appear to men to be fasting, but to your Father who is in secret. And your Father who sees in secret will reward you openly.

Matthew 6:16–18 mev

PRAISE AS A WEAPON

Heavenly Father, my heart and mouth overflow in praises to You! Not just for all the blessings and benefits You provide [see Psalm 68:19 NKJV], but for who You are. I praise You for Your greatness as Creator, and for Your love, power, goodness and mighty acts. I praise You for being my Rescuer, coming through when I've faced seemingly impossible situations. I praise You for sending Jesus Christ to become my Savior, and for sending the Holy Spirit as my Helper. When I am focused on praising You, it sends confusion into the ranks of the enemy! Thank You for this powerful weapon that defeats intimidation the enemy tries to put upon me. Praise will help win the victory in every battle. As long as I have breath in my lungs, I will continue to shout and sing praises to You for Your faithfulness, Almighty God, Maker of heaven and earth, Amen.

Jehoshaphat appointed men to sing to the LORD and to praise him for the splendor of his holiness as they went out at the head of the army, saying: "Give thanks to the LORD, for his love endures forever." As they began to sing and praise, the LORD set ambushes against the men of Ammon and Moab and Mount Seir who were invading Judah, and they were defeated.

2 CHRONICLES 20:21–22

Praise be to the LORD my Rock, who trains my hands for war, my fingers for battle. He is my loving God and my fortress, my stronghold and my deliverer, my shield, in whom I take refuge, who subdues peoples under me.

PSALM 144:1–2

SEEING THE INVISIBLE

*T*hank You, Lord God, that Your Word gives insight into spiritual warfare and shows us this battle is with invisible enemies. Paul calls these hostile forces principalities, rulers of darkness, and spiritual wickedness in high places [see Ephesians 6:12 KJV; 2 Corinthians 10:4–5]. Please sharpen my spiritual vision so I can look past the physical realm and not be blind to what happens in the invisible realm. Teach me how to wield the weapons You provide to demolish demonic strongholds and fight until victory comes. Because Jesus came to destroy the works of the devil, I boldly declare to the enemy that he is a defeated foe [see 1 John 3:8 NKJV]. Help me develop discipline to spend quality time in Your presence and in the Word so that I become a mighty warrior for You. Lord, thank You for the privilege of representing You in this hour, to see Your will done on the earth as it is in heaven, Amen.

"Don't be afraid," the prophet answered. "Those who are with us are more than those who are with them."

*And Elisha prayed, "Open his eyes, L*ORD*, so that he may see." Then the* LORD *opened the servant's eyes, and he looked and saw the hills full of horses and chariots of fire all around Elisha.*

2 KINGS 6:16–17

So we look not at the things which are seen, but at the things which are unseen; for the things which are visible are temporal [just brief and fleeting], but the things which are invisible are everlasting and imperishable.

2 CORINTHIANS 4:18 AMP

Declaration

I declare that I am a child of God. I will serve and honor my loving heavenly Father and Jesus my Savior this day and the rest of my life—regardless of difficulties or distractions. I am determined to pray with power, persistence, praise and discernment to avert the enemy's strategies. Using the authority Jesus provides to me, I will remain vigilant to resist demonic attacks that attempt to divert me from God's divine purpose. I will try to listen more carefully and commit to praying about matters that are on God's heart, as I'm guided by the Holy Spirit. To achieve this, I declare that I will pray in agreement with prayer partners and give thanks and praise to my Savior, Jesus Christ, for shedding His blood for me.

PART 2

Praying AGAINST HINDRANCES

LETTING GO OF UNFORGIVENESS

Father, I know unforgiveness is a hindrance to answered prayer. And I realize I must forgive those who have wounded and betrayed me. Your Word tells me to bless and pray for those who mistreat me [see Luke 6:28]. But my pain is so deep; please, God, give me Your strength to obey You. I refuse to listen when the enemy bombards my mind with memories of the hurts and betrayals I've experienced. So, Lord, as an act of my will—not my emotions—I choose to forgive _____ [insert name or names]. I also resist the desire to get even, leaving the judgment of this person's actions in Your hands. Jesus, thank You that through Your death and resurrection my sins are forgiven. Thank You for healing these wounds and setting me free by the power of Your blood. I receive Your loving pardon and the peace only You can give, wonderful Savior! Amen.

And when you stand praying, if you hold anything against anyone, forgive them, so that your Father in heaven may forgive you your sins.

MARK 11:25

Christ suffered for you, leaving you an example, that you should follow in his steps. "He committed no sin, and no deceit was found in his mouth." When they hurled their insults at him, he did not retaliate; when he suffered, he made no threats. Instead, he entrusted himself to him who judges justly.

1 PETER 2:21–23

AVOIDING DECEPTION

Dear God, I'm concerned to see how easily people can be deceived. When a Christian friend tried to get me to attend a new "secret" religious gathering, I soon realized she was dabbling in one of Satan's counterfeits—the occult. Lord, Your Word forbids such activities, calling them an abomination [see Deuteronomy 7:25 NKJV]. Give me wisdom about how I can warn my friend against getting caught up in teaching that will lead her astray. Lord, please reveal to _____ [name] an understanding of biblical truth about the heresy of the occult and set her free from the darkness it brings. Father, keep me from being deceived or walking in error. Help me always to measure any new doctrines I'm exposed to against the truth of Scripture. I only desire to worship and obey You, my Lord. May I never be gullible enough to embrace false teaching, in Jesus' name, Amen.

There shall not be found among you anyone who ... uses divination, one who practices witchcraft, or one who interprets omens, or a sorcerer, or one who casts a spell, or a medium, or a spiritist, or one who calls up the dead. For whoever does these things is detestable to the LORD.

DEUTERONOMY 18:10–12 NASB

See to it that no one takes you captive through hollow and deceptive philosophy, which depends on human tradition and the elemental spiritual forces of this world rather than on Christ.

COLOSSIANS 2:8

OVERCOMING ANGER

Dear God, please help me control my hot temper. I'm quick to explode in a loud, offensive voice when I hear opinions or see situations I feel are wrong. It's okay to be angry about unjust, evil actions, but to explode with a rude response is not okay [see Ephesians 4:26–27]. I don't want to cooperate with the enemy's camp by not controlling my hateful speech. May the Holy Spirit stop me when I'm about to respond angrily, and also help me guard my words so that I speak only when I'm able to give a reasonable reply. I desire to be compassionate and kind, like You, and cultivate the fruit of the Spirit. I pray the prayer of David, that "the words of my mouth and the meditation of my heart be acceptable in Your sight, O Lord" [Psalm 19:14 NKJV]. Thank You in advance for helping me temper my temper, Amen.

Get rid of all bitterness, rage and anger, brawling and slander, along with every form of malice. Be kind and compassionate to one another, forgiving each other, just as in Christ God forgave you.

Ephesians 4:31–32

My dearest brothers and sisters, take this to heart: Be quick to listen, but slow to speak. And be slow to become angry, for human anger is never a legitimate tool to promote God's righteous purpose.

James 1:19–20 TPT

VICTORY OVER FEAR

Fear! Like a sharp knife, fear has almost paralyzed my emotions, Lord. I fear a stranger on my bus or a suspicious-looking person in the parking lot. I confess that I'm struggling with this attack of fear against my mind. Help me fix my thoughts on the promises in Your Word stating that through Christ, I can triumph over fear. Knowing that Your power is greater than the power of the evil one, I refuse to allow fear of any kind to keep overwhelming me. Lord, I declare that You have not given me "a spirit of fear, but of power and of love and of a sound mind" [2 Timothy 1:7 NKJV]. Help me strengthen my confidence in Your Word so that anxiety cannot overcome me in the days ahead. I choose to praise You in advance for bringing me through to victory, in Jesus' name, Amen.

Do not fear [anything], for I am with you; do not be afraid, for I am your God. I will strengthen you, be assured I will help you; I will certainly take hold of you with My righteous right hand [a hand of justice, of power, of victory, of salvation].

ISAIAH 41:10 AMP

He Himself has said, "I will never leave you nor forsake you." So we may boldly say: "The Lord is my helper; I will not fear. What can man do to me?"

HEBREWS 13:5–6 NKJV

SAYING NO TO WORRY

Lord, forgive me for the times that I allow my mind to be consumed by worrying about people or situations over which I have no control. I bring my concerns and petitions to You in prayer, offering thanks for all the prayers You have answered in the past. And I choose to walk in peace, knowing You are able to do abundantly above what I could ask or think. Right now, I take authority over the enemy, who tries to bombard my mind with anxious thoughts. I say *no* to worry. I stand in faith, believing that I can commit my concerns to You and trust You to intervene according to Your will and Your perfect timing. Even if bad things happen, You are a good Father who can take what the devil means for evil and turn it into good [see Genesis 50:18–21 NKJV]. Thank You for Your love and faithfulness, Lord, Amen.

Do not worry about your life, what you will eat or drink; or about your body, what you will wear. Is not life more than food, and the body more than clothes? Look at the birds of the air; they do not sow or reap or store away in barns, and yet your heavenly Father feeds them. Are you not much more valuable than they? Can any one of you by worrying add a single hour to your life?"

MATTHEW 6:25–27

Do not be anxious about anything, but in every situation, by prayer and petition, with thanksgiving, present your requests to God. And the peace of God, which transcends all understanding, will guard your hearts and your minds in Christ Jesus.

PHILIPPIANS 4:6–7

JUDGING OTHERS

Heavenly Father, I acknowledge that I have a habit of judging others. Even when I don't know the whole truth about a situation, I tend to criticize unfairly those involved. Your Word clearly warns us not to judge, and I know that judgment must be left up to You alone. So I choose no longer to play into the enemy's hand by yielding to this bad habit. I confess that judging others is sinful, and with Your help, I pledge to stop it. I pray that the Holy Spirit will send me a red flag of warning when I'm about to fall into this trap again. Lord, I desire to be pleasing to You and be a good example for others. Please help me renew my mind, control my words and always speak blessings to others. Father, purify my heart, in Jesus' name, Amen.

Do not judge, or you too will be judged. For in the same way you judge others, you will be judged, and with the measure you use, it will be measured to you.

Why do you look at the speck of sawdust in your brother's eye and pay no attention to the plank in your own eye?

MATTHEW 7:1–3

So then, each of us will give account of ourselves to God.

Therefore let us stop passing judgment on one another. Instead, make up your mind not to put any stumbling block or obstacle in the way of a brother or sister.

ROMANS 14:12–13

NO COMPLAINING!

No Complaining Allowed. Lord, I need that sign hung over my thought life! I admit that I'm too often full of sarcasm and criticism. I'm quick to gripe about the weather, the government, the traffic, waiting in line, any unexpected delay I encounter. My criticism often includes my neighbors, my bills, my boss, even my kids. O God, please help me overcome my negative thoughts and words about matters I can't control. When I learn about policies I disagree with, give me grace to intercede about the matter instead of complaining. When I run into sudden delays, help me pray for those involved instead of criticizing them. Since I want to develop an attitude of gratitude, I will start by counting my blessings and thanking You daily for the wonderful things I do have and do enjoy about my life. My list of blessings consists of _____ and _____ and _____ [list your blessings]. Thank You, Lord, Amen.

*Praise the L*ORD*, my soul, and forget not all his benefits—who forgives all your sins and heals all your diseases, who redeems your life from the pit and crowns you with love and compassion, who satisfies your desires with good things so that your youth is renewed like the eagle's.*

PSALM 103:2–5

Do not let any unwholesome talk come out of your mouths, but only what is helpful for building others up according to their needs, that it may benefit those who listen.

EPHESIANS 4:29

YIELDING TO TEMPTATION

God, please help me break the habit of giving in to temptation, doing things I know are wrong. It's so easy to say "the devil made me do it" when I fail like this. I need Your strength to cast down "every high thing that exalts itself against the knowledge of God, bringing every thought into captivity to the obedience of Christ" [2 Corinthians 10:5 NKJV]. Please help me correct my wrong thinking and ungodly actions. Show me the root of my compulsive behavior and strengthen me to overcome it. As I stand against the enemy to break my pattern of bad habits, lead me to people to whom I can be accountable—friends, a counselor or a support group. My spirit is willing, but my body is weak [see Matthew 26:41]. Jesus, I'm trusting You to truly set me free by the power of Your blood, Amen.

Therefore, I urge you, brothers and sisters, in view of God's mercy, to offer your bodies as a living sacrifice, holy and pleasing to God—this is your true and proper worship. Do not conform any longer to the pattern of this world, but be transformed by the renewing of your mind. Then you will be able to test and approve what God's will is—his good, pleasing and perfect will.

ROMANS 12:1–2

Whatever is true, whatever is noble, whatever is right, whatever is pure, whatever is lovely, whatever is admirable—if anything is excellent or praiseworthy—think about such things. Whatever you have learned or received or heard from me, or seen in me [Paul]—put it into practice. And the God of peace will be with you.

PHILIPPIANS 4:8–9

DEFEATING SELFISHNESS

Lord Jesus, You know all about my stubborn, selfish nature. For too long I've lived for my own pleasure and rebelled against Your ways. When I've put myself on the throne instead of You, selfish ambition has kept me from experiencing Your best. When the Holy Spirit warned me of my pushy ego, I didn't listen—not realizing I was aiding the enemy. I am so sorry! Please forgive me and help me abstain from self-centeredness. I truly desire to be more loving, caring and concerned for others as You lead me to those whom I can bless with a prayer or an encouraging word. Thank You for being my Savior, Lord and King, Amen.

Do nothing out of selfish ambition or vain conceit. Rather, in humility value others above yourselves, not looking to your own interests but each of you to the interests of the others.

PHILIPPIANS 2:3–4

But if you harbor bitter envy and selfish ambition in your hearts, do not boast about it or deny the truth. Such "wisdom" does not come down from heaven but is earthly, unspiritual, demonic.

JAMES 3:14–15

RESISTING GOD'S GUIDANCE

Dear Jesus, You know all about my tendency to resist following Your ways, usually for selfish reasons or fear of the future. I've too easily put my own desires on the throne of my life instead of choosing Your will for me. I am so sorry. Lord, please forgive me. Strengthen me to resist the enemy, abstain from self-centeredness and follow Your example of humility. Help me never forget that You know the end from the beginning. I'm so thankful that You have never failed me yet, and You are completely trustworthy. Help me reach out to others with care and concern. May the Holy Spirit keep me sensitive to those who need my help and guide me in ways to respond in kindness. Thank You for being my faithful Shepherd, Lord and King, Amen.

Make God the utmost delight and pleasure of your life, and he will provide for you what you desire the most. Give God the right to direct your life, and as you trust him along the way you'll find he pulled it off perfectly!

Psalm 37:4–5 tpt

For the Lord God is a sun and shield; the Lord will give grace and glory; no good thing will He withhold from those who walk uprightly.
  O Lord of hosts, blessed is the man who trusts in You!

Psalm 84:11–12 nkjv

SIN PATTERNS THAT HARASS

*L*ord Jesus, thank You for redeeming us from the curse of the law of sin and death by becoming a curse for us. In Your mercy, please deliver us from these sinful patterns that have caused pain and have harassed our family for years. Scripture reveals that various unhealthy habits such as lying, adultery, defiant attitudes—even a bent toward certain peculiarities—have been passed down through the generations [see Exodus 20:3–6]. I know Satan strives to keep some family members in bondage to these unrighteous traits. But Your blood sacrifice can wipe them clean, bringing deliverance, healing and wholeness. Now I trust You to give us victory over those negative traits that are not pleasing to You. I declare that they are uprooted and cast out, in Your name. I give You praise for the blessings and positive attributes that have come from my ancestry. Thank You for Your faithfulness, Lord, Amen.

Christ purchased our freedom and redeemed us from the curse of the Law and its condemnation by becoming a curse for us—for it is written, "Cursed is everyone who hangs [crucified] on a tree (cross)."

GALATIANS 3:13 AMP

But Scripture has locked up everything under the control of sin, so that what was promised, being given through faith in Jesus Christ, might be given to those who believe.

GALATIANS 3:22

CONQUERING SHAME

Heavenly Father, I am so burdened with shame; I feel unworthy even to approach You in prayer. My secret sin, committed some time ago, still torments me in the night. I feel dirty, ashamed and guilt-ridden. Even though I have accepted Jesus as my Savior, I can't forgive myself or forget my past. Please heal my memories and renew my mind. I declare that the enemy cannot continue tormenting me with accusations and flashbacks to my previous lifestyle. I tell shame to be gone, washed away by the blood of Jesus Christ. Help me now see myself as You see me, Lord. Thank You for restoring my dignity. I am so thankful that Jesus paid the price for my sins when He went to the cross. I humbly receive the forgiveness He bought for me. May I live a life worthy of Your love, forever free of shame and guilt, Amen.

Who is a God like you, who pardons sin and forgives . . . ? You do not stay angry forever but delight to show mercy. You will again have compassion on us; you will tread our sins underfoot and hurl our iniquities into the depths of the sea.

Micah 7:18–19

For it is with your heart that you believe and are justified, and it is with your mouth that you profess your faith and are saved. As Scripture says, "Anyone who believes in him will never be put to shame."

Romans 10:10–11

BALANCING PRIORITIES

Lord, I'm trying my best to balance all my tasks, but it's hard to avoid feeling pressured. Sometimes it seems there's not enough of me to go around in meeting all the demands. Both my energy and the clock run out before I can get it all done. And when I get frazzled, the people I love most receive the brunt of my frustration. Jesus, I want to draw from Your peace and strength to do the most necessary things first. And to put lesser things on my "later" list, which will always be there tomorrow. Please guide me in always using my tongue wisely and with kindness [see Proverbs 31:26]. Keep me from falling into the enemy's trap by overdoing and getting stressed out. Lord, I trust You to help me find stability and balance in keeping my priorities straight. Thank You, Lord, Amen.

See then that you walk circumspectly, not as fools but as wise, redeeming the time, because the days are evil.

Therefore do not be unwise, but understand what the will of the Lord is.

EPHESIANS 5:15–17 NKJV

Whatever you do, work at it with all your heart, as working for the Lord, not for human masters, since you know that you will receive an inheritance from the Lord as a reward.

COLOSSIANS 3:23–24

Declaration

I declare today that no weakness or hindrance that I need to overcome will keep me from pressing through to see my prayers answered. No obstacle the enemy puts in my path—unforgiveness, fear, worry, shame, judging, anger—will stop me from seeing victory in these spiritual battles. I decree that I am seated with Christ in the heavenly realm of authority, and I can approach God's throne with confidence and receive mercy and grace in time of need [see Ephesians 2:6 TPT; Hebrews 4:15–16]. As I spend time in the Word and allow the Holy Spirit to guide me and perfect me, I will triumph over the adversary, who is a defeated foe. I lift my praises to God, who alone is worthy to receive all glory and honor forever!

PART 3

Praying FOR LIFE'S MILESTONES

GRADUATION

Graduation! Thank You, Lord, for helping me reach this significant milestone. Hard work and sacrifice paid off, but I couldn't have achieved this without Your constant guidance. Thank You for family and friends who encouraged me and prayed me through to this big day. Bless them. Now guide me into a career opening where I can best use my education and training, and protect me from accepting the wrong job. Give me favor to find employment at a place where I can grow and be of help to others. Thank You for the talents You've given me and for the destiny You planned for me even before I was born. I declare that the enemy cannot interfere with Your plan, and with the help of the Holy Spirit, I will fulfill it. Lord, I give You praise for the wonderful life You have prepared for me, Amen.

The LORD will accomplish that which concerns me; Your [unwavering] lovingkindness, O LORD, endures forever—do not abandon the works of Your own hands.

PSALM 138:8 AMP

Trust in the LORD with all your heart, and lean not on your own understanding; in all your ways acknowledge Him, and He shall direct your paths.

Do not be wise in your own eyes; fear the LORD and depart from evil.

PROVERBS 3:5–7 NKJV

ENGAGEMENT

Lord, he wants me to marry him. To spend the rest of my life with him. How blessed and excited I am! Will I make a good wife? Will I be able to adjust to married life after all these years of singleness? Help me. Teach me. Send a mentor to guide me on this new adventure. Whether she is a woman who has a successful marriage or a widow with wise experience, her input could be so helpful to me. Be with us Lord, as _____ [name] and I plan our wedding and our future together so that they bring honor to You. If the enemy tries to cause conflict between us or between our families, help us resolve the issues with Your loving guidance. Thank You, Lord, for giving us Your blessing in this season of our lives, Amen.

May the favor of the Lord our God rest on us; establish the work of our hands for us—yes, establish the work of our hands.

Psalm 90:17

Love is patient, love is kind. It does not envy, it does not boast, it is not proud. It does not dishonor others, it is not self-seeking, it is not easily angered, it keeps no record of wrongs. Love does not delight in evil but rejoices with the truth. It always protects, always trusts, always hopes, always perseveres.

1 Corinthians 13:4–7

THE WEDDING

Lord, I have dreamed about this day since I was a little girl. My wedding. Marrying my love, my sweet best friend. I pray that our deep love for You and for each other will be so evident when we exchange vows. May I radiate Your inner beauty as I walk down the aisle to join my groom. So many friends and family to greet. Thank You for each one who helped make this wonderful wedding possible. Thank You for the special honeymoon _____ [name] and I will share together. I am so excited to begin my new adventure with this special man You have given me. May we find ways to blend our different backgrounds into a covenant relationship of love and respect that the enemy cannot sever. Bless our marriage and help us be a blessing to each other, Amen.

But at the beginning of creation God "made them male and female." "For this reason a man will leave his father and mother and be united to his wife, and the two will become one flesh." So they are no longer two, but one flesh. Therefore what God has joined together, let no one separate.

MARK 10:6–9

The man who finds a wife finds a treasure, and he receives favor from the LORD.

PROVERBS 18:22 NLT

MY FIRSTBORN

Lord, how wonderful to be a mother! Thank You for this beautiful baby put in my arms today. How precious is Your gift of life. I count her little toes. I marvel at her sweet mouth. I smother her with kisses. So tiny, vulnerable and dependent on us. Make me a capable, wise mother. Give _____ [father's name] and me wisdom as we raise this child. Please protect her from sickness, accidents or any plan of the enemy to harm her. So much of life is ahead for all of us. We're trusting You to help us make wise decisions that will affect our daughter's future. Guide me in modeling Your ways so _____ [child's name] will develop a lifelong love of and devotion to You, dear Lord. Thank You that You have trusted me to be a mom. I love You, Amen.

A woman giving birth to a child has pain because her time has come; but when her baby is born she forgets the anguish because of her joy that a child is born into the world.

JOHN 16:21

Train up a child in the way he should go [teaching him to seek God's wisdom and will for his abilities and talents], even when he is old he will not depart from it.

PROVERBS 22:6 AMP

A BRAND-NEW YEAR

Father God, thank You for another birthday—a brand-new year ahead. Some women count their wrinkles or gray hairs. I count my blessings. Thank You for my health, my family, my friends, my home, my church, my food and my other provisions. I never want to take these for granted. You have been a faithful Provider over the years. I give You thanks for helping me through the challenges I faced last year to reach this milestone. Also for the lessons learned, for historic events, and for fun and happy memories I will cherish always. Lord, I dedicate the year ahead to You, and I declare that no evil weapon formed against me will prosper. I trust You to help me be salt and light to the people You bring across my path. In Jesus' name, Amen.

Because of the Lord's great love we are not consumed, for his compassions never fail. They are new every morning; great is your faithfulness. I say to myself, "The Lord is my portion; therefore I will wait for him."

Lamentations 3:22–24

The Lord is my shepherd; I shall not want. He makes me to lie down in green pastures; He leads me beside the still waters. He restores my soul; He leads me in the paths of righteousness for His name's sake....

... Surely goodness and mercy shall follow me all the days of my life; and I will dwell in the house of the Lord forever.

Psalm 23:1–3, 6 nkjv

MOVING AGAIN

Lord, our family is moving again. Please help us transition from the life we've gotten used to here, to the many unknowns that lie ahead. I'm sad to leave behind our neighbors, church friends and the town and home we settled in years ago. It's hard to say goodbye. But I see Your hand in this: _____ [list positive circumstances like "a promotion for my husband," "living closer to family," "better educational and job prospects for our children," etc.]. Knowing You will go before us and guide us through uncharted waters takes fear out of the venture. Thank You for directing us to a new home, new friends and a new church family. Help all of us deal with emotionally letting go and moving forward. May Your angels protect us and our belongings as we make this move. Thank You for preparing our family for what lies ahead in the new place, Amen.

*"For in him we live and move and have our being."
As some of your own poets have said, "We are his
offspring."*

ACTS 17:28

*If you say, "The LORD is my refuge," and you make
the Most High your dwelling . . . he will command
his angels concerning you to guard you in all your
ways.*

PSALM 91:9, 11

MAKING OUR HOUSE A HOME

Lord God, a home at last! I'm so grateful for this new place You have provided for us. Help me create a loving home that reflects our family's personalities and tastes, and is pleasing to You. Guard us from overspending as we furnish and decorate it. Stir up the gift of hospitality in me, that I may serve well my family and any guests You choose to send. May ours be a home of comfort, healing, friendship, rest and encouragement. One where we enjoy fun and memorable celebrations. Help us make our home a shelter of safety and peace. Lord, please station Your holy angels about our dwelling and over our property to keep evil forces away. I pray that the Holy Spirit will be an ever-present Guest in this place. I ask in the name of Jesus, my Savior, Amen.

*The curse of the L*ORD *is on the house of the wicked, but He blesses the home of the just and righteous.*

PROVERBS 3:33 AMP

My people will live in peaceful dwelling places, in secure homes, in undisturbed places of rest.

ISAIAH 32:18

MY NEST IS EMPTY

Lord, I miss my children since they've all left home. Where did the years go? Now they're off to college or distant jobs, and our house is strangely quiet. When the phone rings, I hope it's one of them calling home. For too long, I've let my identity be wrapped up in being their mom. Show me what's next, Lord. Where do I direct my experience, talent and skills? Do I take a class or teach a class? Start a prayer group? Volunteer someplace? Go back to a secular job? Lord, help me discern Your leading for my life at this milestone. Keep me from falling into the enemy's trap of wasting time with meaningless activity or joining gossipy groups. When a door of opportunity seems to open, please confirm whether it is Your best for me. Thank You, Lord, for helping me be patient and wait for Your direction, Amen.

Take hold of my instructions; don't let them go. Guard them, for they are the key to life.

Don't do as the wicked do, and don't follow the path of evildoers. Don't even think about it; don't go that way. Turn away and keep moving.

PROVERBS 4:13–15 NLT

For the wise, these proverbs will make you even wiser, and for those with discernment, you will be able to acquire brilliant strategies for leadership.

PROVERBS 1:5 TPT

MOTHER-IN-LAW PRAYER

*L*ord, thank You for my child, _____ [name], and for his/her spouse, _____ [name]. Help me love and accept my son-in-law/daughter-in-law just as he/she is. When I am inclined to judge or criticize, remind me to hold my tongue and trust You to intervene in the matter. I tend to overlook my own child's weaknesses where his/her spouse is involved. When either one of them asks for advice, give me godly wisdom and discretion about how to respond. Lord, I truly want to love _____ [name] with Your love. Enable me to be a good parent-in-law. Show me how to pray more effectively for my son-in-law/daughter-in-law and affirm his/her good qualities much more often. Thank You for strengthening this marriage and protecting them from the enemy's effort to bring discord into their relationship. I ask this in Your holy name, Amen.

Now that you have purified yourselves by obeying the truth so that you have sincere love for each other, love one another deeply, from the heart. For you have been born again, not of perishable seed, but of imperishable, through the living and enduring word of God.

1 Peter 1:22–23

Follow God's example, therefore, as dearly loved children and walk in the way of love, just as Christ loved us and gave himself up for us as a fragrant offering and sacrifice to God.

Ephesians 5:1–2

NOW I'M A GRANDMOTHER

*L*ord, I praise You for the gift of grandchildren. It is such a wonderful time in life to enjoy these children, but not to have the full responsibility for them. Help me be a good example and a fun granny to them. Make me sensitive to particular needs they may have, so I can pray more specifically for each one. Help me not to play favorites among my grandkids. Lord, please make it possible for me to have special alone times with them—either individually or in groups—like sleepovers, field trips or picnics in the park. Even if they move away from my area, I trust You to make a way for fun visits to happen. Give me wisdom to be the grandmother who will be a help—not a hindrance—to them and their parents. Bless them with Your love. May guardian angels protect and watch over them, Amen.

For I will pour water on the thirsty land, and streams on the dry ground; I will pour out my Spirit on your offspring, and my blessing on your descendants. They will spring up like grass in a meadow, like poplar trees by flowing streams.

Isaiah 44:3–4

I constantly remember you in my prayers. . . . I am reminded of your sincere faith, which first lived in your grandmother Lois and in your mother Eunice and, I am persuaded, now lives in you also.

2 Timothy 1:3, 5

CHRISTMAS REMEMBRANCES

Dear Jesus, what a glorious time of year it is when we stop to celebrate Your birth. Though the world has greatly commercialized the season, this special holiday bears Your name. Help me, by example, to teach my children and grandchildren the importance of honoring You on this day we set aside to remember Your birthday. Bless the families who gather to enjoy the holiday together. And for those who have conflicts and tensions among them, help them make peace with one another. May my family boldly share with others the real meaning of Christmas by how we act and what we say. I pray that multitudes around the world will receive You as Savior and Lord during this memorable time. Christmas truly is a yearly milestone for me. Thank You, Jesus, for coming to earth as the promised Messiah to become our Redeemer, Amen.

For to us a child is born, to us a son is given, and the government will be on his shoulders. And he will be called Wonderful Counselor, Mighty God, Everlasting Father, Prince of Peace. Of the greatness of his government and peace there will be no end.

ISAIAH 9:6–7

An angel of the Lord appeared to [Joseph] in a dream and said, "... She will give birth to a son, and you are to give him the name Jesus, because he will save his people from their sins."

All this took place to fulfill what the Lord had said through the prophet: "The virgin will conceive and will give birth to a son, and they will call him Immanuel" (which means "God with us").

MATTHEW 1:20–23

EASTER CELEBRATION

*L*ord, how I love this marvelous season when we celebrate Your resurrection. Thank You, Jesus, for Your willingness to die on the cross for my sins. And thank You for coming back from death to give us new life. I regret how so many people focus on bunnies, Easter eggs and chocolates instead of on You. Lord, I want to keep Your sacrifice of love and the miracle of Your resurrection foremost in my heart. Give me opportunities to share with others the true significance of Resurrection Sunday. Because You arose from the dead, Satan's defeat is certain, and the curse of the law of sin and death is broken [see Romans 8:2; 1 John 3:8]. What a blessing to be able to celebrate with my family and church friends as we greet one another: "He is risen! He is risen indeed!" All praise, honor and glory belong to You, our risen Savior, Amen.

The angel said to the women, "Do not be afraid, for I know that you are looking for Jesus, who was crucified. He is not here; he has risen, just as he said. Come and see the place where he lay. Then go quickly and tell his disciples: 'He has risen from the dead and is going ahead of you into Galilee. There you will see him.' Now I have told you."

Matthew 28:5–7

So the women hurried away from the tomb, afraid yet filled with joy, and ran to tell his disciples. Suddenly Jesus met them. "Greetings," he said. They came to him, clasped his feet and worshiped him. Then Jesus said to them, "Do not be afraid. Go and tell my brothers to go to Galilee; there they will see me."

Mathew 28:8–10

Declaration

I lift up praises to my loving Father God for blessing me with many special milestones in my life. His faithfulness has surpassed my dreams, far exceeding what I could have hoped for. He has walked with me through happy and challenging days, always working for my best interests against the enemy's strategies. I am thankful that the Lord's favor, grace, love, comfort, compassion and protection have overshadowed me. Grateful for the people, experiences and places that have greatly impacted me, I speak blessings over those who have walked some of those paths with me. May God reward each one as only He can. I decree that I will successfully make it through whatever unexpected bends in the road I may face. The Holy Spirit will be my forever Guide and Comforter.

PART 4

Praying for CHILDREN & GRANDCHILDREN

LORD, GIVE US CHILDREN!

Heavenly Father, You see our empty arms, our empty cradle. You know our deep desire to have a child, whether by birth or adoption. _____ [husband's name] and I submit our wills to You and trust Your plan for us. During our waiting time, help us prepare to become good parents. We will not allow the enemy's voice of discouragement to rob our hope. We continue to trust You to bless us with one or more children to love and nurture. You alone are the source of all life, and we will always thank You for this incredible gift. We bring this request in the wonderful name of Jesus, Your own Son, who Himself came into the world as a baby, Amen.

He settles the childless woman in her home as a happy mother of children.
  Praise the Lord.

Psalm 113:9

I prayed for this child, and the Lord has granted me what I asked of him. So now I give him to the Lord. For his whole life he will be given over to the Lord.

1 Samuel 1:27–28

FOR THE CHILD IN MY WOMB

Lord, I'm pregnant! Oh, thank You for this child in my womb. Even from this early stage of life, may my baby feel my love and acceptance, and be overshadowed by Your protection. Guide me with wisdom as to what I eat and how I discipline my body for the sake of this little one. Also guide the prayers I will pray for the precious life inside me. I trust You to help me carry this child to full term and have a safe delivery. Be with the doctors, nurses and all who will be involved in caring for me and for our baby. Help _____ [husband's name] and me prepare our home to receive this gift. I'm so excited. Thank You so much, Lord, for trusting me to be a mom, Amen.

I praise you because I am fearfully and wonderfully made; your works are wonderful, I know that full well. My frame was not hidden from you when I was made in the secret place, when I was woven together in the depths of the earth.

PSALM 139:14–15

Your eyes saw my unformed body; all the days ordained for me were written in your book before one of them came to be. How precious to me are your thoughts, God!

PSALM 139:16–17

FOR HEALTH AND PROTECTION

Thank You, Lord, that You station angels about my children to protect them from harm in all their ways. Please guard them from wrong influences, wrong friends and a wrong environment that would cause any one of them to veer off course. I stand against the strategy of the enemy to deceive their minds about the depth of Your love for them. Keep them from embracing the world's views that are contrary to Your truth, or from pursuing self-destructive activities. Bring godly friends into their lives at the right time who can strengthen their walk with You. I pray that in all respects, You will sustain them with good health in body, soul and spirit. Help me teach them by example to cast all their cares on You [see 1 Peter 5:7]. Thank You for Your constant loving care for my children, in Jesus' name, Amen.

But let all who take refuge in you be glad; let them ever sing for joy. Spread your protection over them, that those who love your name may rejoice in you.

PSALM 5:11

For he will command his angels concerning you to guard you in all your ways; they will lift you in their hands, so that you will not strike your foot against a stone.

PSALM 91:11–12

FOR MY SPECIAL-NEEDS CHILD

*L*ord, every life is precious to You, no matter the person's level of health or beauty in the world's eyes. I cherish my special-needs child, _____ [name], as a treasured gift from You. Despite his challenges and disabilities, his sweet smile and personality have endeared him to many people. Give my husband and me great wisdom to make right decisions in matters concerning our son. I also pray that those helping him—doctors, therapists, technicians, special education teachers, friends—will show wisdom and compassion. I pray _____ [name] will experience Your love in tangible ways. Please protect him from suffering the pain of rejection or bullying. Help him rise above the limited judgments people place on him, so he can fulfill Your plan for his life. May he be a joy and inspiration to others, as he is to our family. I ask this in the mighty name of Jesus, Amen.

See that you do not despise one of these little ones. For I tell you that their angels in heaven always see the face of my Father in heaven.

MATTHEW 18:10

Then people brought little children to Jesus for him to place his hands on them and pray for them. . . .
Jesus said, "Let the little children come to me, and do not hinder them, for the kingdom of heaven belongs to such as these." When he had placed his hands on them, he went on from there.

MATTHEW 19:13–15

FOR MY NEWLY ADOPTED CHILD

Father, thank You for the opportunity You've given me to be mother to this precious child—such a wonderful gift! Help me be a godly mother and always keep the lines of communication open between us. May _____ [child's name] never feel abandoned or rejected, but know the depth of my love. I hold this child in my heart as though I had given birth, and I dedicate her to You. Please give me Your wisdom and guidance to be the best mom I can possibly be. Bless this special daughter of mine with good health and a deep understanding of Your never-failing love. Give _____ [name] the assurance that my arms and home are always open to her. Protect her from any illnesses or evil influences related to her biological parents. Thank You that they chose life for their child, and I pray Your blessings upon them, Amen.

A father to orphans and an advocate for widows is God in his holy dwelling place. God causes the lonely to dwell in families.

Psalm 68:5–6 isv

But you received the Spirit of adoption by whom we cry out, "Abba, Father." The Spirit Himself bears witness with our spirit that we are children of God, and if children, then heirs—heirs of God and joint heirs with Christ.

Romans 8:15–17 nkjv

MY CHILD IS SICK

Lord Jesus, You cared enough about little children to touch and heal them when You walked the earth. My child is suddenly sick and urgently needs Your soothing touch. I know You can heal _____ [name] miraculously. Or You can use highly trained medical teams. So I ask You to guide my husband and me to the right doctor, the right diagnosis, the right treatment. Give us wisdom for all the decisions we will face in our search. Help me get the word out to faithful friends who will stand with us in prayer during this unsettling time. O Great Physician, we need You to intervene, touch, heal, restore _____ [name] to health. I renounce a spirit of fear the enemy would try to bring upon us. Thank You for giving me Your peace as I place my child into Your loving care. Lord, I trust You completely, Amen.

And wherever he [Jesus] went—into villages, towns or countryside—they placed the sick in the marketplaces. They begged him to let them touch even the edge of his cloak, and all who touched it were healed.

MARK 6:56

Jesus called his twelve disciples to him and gave them authority to drive out impure spirits and to heal every disease and sickness.

MATTHEW 10:1

FOR MY STEPCHILDREN

Lord, You know how inadequate I feel for taking on the responsibility of helping care for my husband's children from a previous marriage. I know that whether breakups are caused by death, divorce or abandonment, the children suffer emotionally. Please shield these children from feeling they are somehow responsible for what happened in the loss of their mom. That's a lie the enemy uses to harass them and bring them into the bondage of shame and guilt. Father, _____ [husband's name] and I need Your great wisdom to provide a peaceful, loving home where his kids can heal and feel safe. Help me assure them that, although I can't take their mom's place, I want to earn their trust with my love and support. Protect our blended family from division and strife. May we always keep the lines of communication open so problems can be resolved without delay. Thank You, Lord, Amen.

If it is possible, as far as it depends on you, live at peace with everyone.

ROMANS 12:18

"For I know the plans I have for you," declares the LORD, "plans to prosper you and not to harm you, plans to give you hope and a future."

JEREMIAH 29:11

FOR MY WAYWARD CHILD

Father, I know that even now, while my child is in the enemy's camp, You love him more than I do. You have a way of escape for him. I'm standing on Your hope-filled Scriptures as I fight this battle in the spiritual realm. Lead someone to help him escape the darkness. May the Holy Spirit give him a desire to return to You, as You reveal to him the depths of Your love. Forgive me for judging him harshly with my negative words. Help me keep a forgiving heart, like the father in Luke 15 who embraced and forgave his son after the prodigal came to his senses and returned to his father's house. Lord, I'm trusting You that someday soon, my son will call on You for help and run into my arms. Thank You, Lord, for breaking every chain of bondage in his life. In Jesus' name, Amen.

*I will contend with those who contend with you, and your children I will save. . . . I, the L*ORD*, am your Savior, your Redeemer, the Mighty One of Jacob.*

ISAIAH 49:25–26

When he came to his senses, he said, " . . . I will set out and go back to my father, and say to him: Father, I have sinned against heaven and against you. . . ." So he got up and went to his father.

But while he was still a long way off, his father saw him and was filled with compassion for him; he ran to his son, threw his arms around him and kissed him. . . .

. . . So they began to celebrate.

LUKE 15:17–18, 20, 24

EDUCATION AND CAREER CHOICES

Lord, please direct my children's decisions as they choose the college or vocational school where they can be trained and develop their talents more fully. Help them find financial favor for scholarships or grants to cover tuition and school expenses. Give them wisdom, understanding and discernment for the choices facing them: courses, teachers, friends, jobs, living arrangements. I pray that they will have good instructors who will not indoctrinate them with an anti-God point of view. Help my children stay strong in their relationships with You, and guide them to a church or fellowship where they can worship with other believers. I pray they will be bold in reaching out to their fellow students and sharing their faith. Please keep the enemy from confusing and distracting them as they study and prepare for their life's work. Thank You, Lord, for answering this mother's prayer, Amen.

Praise the Lord!

How joyful are those who fear the Lord and delight in obeying his commands. Their children will be successful everywhere; an entire generation of godly people will be blessed.

Psalm 112:1–2 nlt

For I will give you words and wisdom that none of your adversaries will be able to resist or contradict.

Luke 21:15

FOR INCREASE AND FAVOR

Father, I pray that my children will keep increasing in their mental, physical, spiritual and social development. May they find favor with You, their instructors and the people they will influence. Help them continue gaining spiritual wisdom and understanding that will aid them in whatever circumstances they may face. Counter the attacks of the enemy that would try to lure them into sin. Lord, help me be a good example to them, and help me always be available when they need my help, advice or prayers. Give them a deep desire to share Your love with their peers, and please You above pleasing themselves or those around them. Thank You, Lord, for enriching my life with the children You have given me. I pray they will each fulfill the destiny for which You created them, Amen.

And Jesus increased in wisdom and stature, and in favor with God and men.

LUKE 2:52 NKJV

We have not stopped praying for you. We continually ask God to fill you with the knowledge of his will through all the wisdom and understanding that the Spirit gives, so that you may live a life worthy of the Lord and please him in every way: bearing fruit in every good work, growing in the knowledge of God.

COLOSSIANS 1:9–10

FOR MY CHILDREN'S FUTURE MATES

Heavenly Father, I pray You'll guide each of my children to know Your will in choosing his/her future mate. Bring each of my children together in Your perfect timing with a young person who knows Jesus as his/her personal Lord and Savior. May each couple have compatible goals for their future, using their talents wisely in the best way possible. May they enjoy doing things together and be encouragers of one another. Help them love each other with a faithful, undying love for as long as they both shall live. When the enemy attempts to bring division and hurt, help them resolve their differences peacefully, with love and respect. May they establish their home according to Your order, Lord. Then help them be good parents, good providers and good examples to their children. Most of all, I pray that they will love You with all their heart, soul, mind and strength, Amen.

Enjoy life with the woman whom you love all the days of your fleeting life which He has given to you under the sun; for this is your reward in life.

ECCLESIASTES 9:9 NASB

An excellent wife, who can find? For her worth is far above jewels. The heart of her husband trusts in her, and he will have no lack of gain. She does him good and not evil all the days of her life.

PROVERBS 31:10–12 NASB

FOR MY ADULT CHILDREN

Lord, help my adult children and their spouses find favor with their employers and colleagues. May they be reliable employees—showing honesty, integrity and the motivation to excel. Help them learn to balance work concerns with home and leisure time. May they be wise and faithful spouses and parents, responsible to take care of their health—body, mind and spirit. Give them Your wisdom in handling financial matters and acting honorably in everything they do. Help them recognize the enemy's attacks against them, and give them Your strategy to thwart those attempts to wreak havoc in their lives. Lord, help me be a faithful prayer warrior for them, sensitive to the Holy Spirit's nudging when immediate prayer is needed. May they be good witnesses for You both at work and elsewhere. Thank You, loving and faithful God, Amen.

I pray that from his glorious, unlimited resources he will empower you with inner strength through his Spirit. Then Christ will make his home in your hearts as you trust in him. Your roots will grow down into God's love and keep you strong. And may you have the power to understand, as all God's people should, how wide, how long, how high, and how deep his love is.

Ephesians 3:16–18 nlt

Blessed are those who fear the Lord, who find great delight in his commands.

Their children will be mighty in the land; the generation of the upright will be blessed. Wealth and riches are in their houses, and their righteousness endures forever.

Psalm 112:1–3

FOR MY GRANDCHILDREN

Lord Jesus, give me creative ideas for imparting spiritual truths to my grandchildren. I desire that each one will choose to make You his/her Savior and live to please You. May they comprehend how deeply Father God loves them, instead of thinking the Christian faith is a list of dos and don'ts. Show me how I can bless them, encourage them and be available for them. Also show me strategies for how to pray for the spiritual, physical and emotional well-being of each one. Please keep them from being deceived by the enemy or walking in error. I want to convey a godly legacy to them when we communicate in phone calls, texts, emails, even handwritten letters. May the seeds of prayer I've planted for them bring a harvest of blessing in their lives now and even after I'm gone. Thank You, Lord, for helping me achieve this desire, Amen.

One generation commends your works to another; they tell of your mighty acts. They speak of the glorious splendor of your majesty. . . . They tell of the power of your awesome works—and I will proclaim your great deeds.

PSALM 145: 4–6

Know therefore that the LORD your God is God; he is the faithful God, keeping his covenant of love to a thousand generations of those who love him and keep his commandments.

DEUTERONOMY 7:9

Declaration

I declare that my children will see the light of the Gospel of Christ. They shall be taught of the Lord, and great will be their peace [see Isaiah 54:13]. The Lord will guide them in paths of righteousness for His name's sake, and goodness and mercy will follow them all the days of their lives [see Psalm 23:3, 6]. In the name and under the authority of Jesus Christ, my Lord, I forbid all powers of evil from exerting influence over my children and grandchildren. I come against any spirits of witchcraft, mind control, occult activity, ungodly music, lust, perversion, rebellion, rejection, suicide, anger, hatred, unforgiveness, bitterness, pride, deception, unbelief, fear, greed, addictions and other snares trying to lure them away from God. I declare the enemy's power is null and void, and all assignments against my children and grandchildren are canceled by the blood of Jesus Christ [see Ephesians 6:12; Deuteronomy 7:25–26; 18:10–12]. I release them to be all that God created them to be!

PART 5

Praying for FAMILY & FRIENDS

PRAYER FOR UNSAVED LOVED ONES

Father God, my heart is burdened for members of my family who don't know You. The busyness of life, disappointments and setbacks, or desires to pursue other interests have separated them from You. I bring them before You now, Lord: _____ and _____ [names]. I pray You'll reveal Your love to them and create in them a hunger for spiritual truth. I stand against the enemy, who has caused them to embrace a lie. They are blind to the reality that You came to set them free and to provide abundant life. Please send across their paths people who will speak into their lives with love, truth, power and conviction. Give me a clear prayer strategy, Lord, and show me creative ways to express my love and concern for them. I give You thanks in advance for the answers I expect to see in days ahead. In Jesus' name, Amen.

The god of this age has blinded the minds of unbelievers, so that they cannot see the light of the gospel that displays the glory of Christ, who is the image of God.

2 Corinthians 4:4

The Lord is not slack concerning His promise, as some count slackness, but is longsuffering toward us, not willing that any should perish but that all should come to repentance.

2 Peter 3:9 nkjv

PRAYER FOR MY HUSBAND

Thank You, Lord, for _____ [husband's name], the life partner You've given me, and for the years we've had together. Help us build a strong, happy marriage as we serve You and seek Your blessings on our family. May we always communicate with one another honestly and lovingly in resolving differences, while giving one another the benefit of the doubt. Thank You that my husband has favor with his boss and co-workers at the job You have provided. I pray You will open opportunities for him to advance so that his skills can best be used. Help him father our children well, assuring them of his unconditional love for them even when discipline is necessary. I stand against any effort by the enemy to bring discord and division into our family. I declare that our home will be a sanctuary where Your presence dwells. I praise You for this, Amen.

"For this reason a man will leave his father and mother and be united to his wife, and the two will become one flesh." This is a profound mystery—but I am talking about Christ and the church. However, each one of you also must love his wife as he loves himself, and the wife must respect her husband.

EPHESIANS 5:31–33

Above all, have fervent and unfailing love for one another, because love covers a multitude of sins [it overlooks unkindness and unselfishly seeks the best for others].

1 PETER 4:8 AMP

FOR MY HUSBAND'S CAREER

Lord, my husband needs Your help so much today. He faces a big challenge at work, where his superiors will be evaluating his job performance. This could affect his future at the company. Please give him the right words to use and the courage to speak with boldness and confidence. May he find favor and fair-minded consideration with the decision-makers. In the name of Jesus, I say *no* to confusion, misunderstanding or any other enemy attempts to disrupt this meeting. Lord, give _____ [husband's name] assurance that, with Your help, we will make it regardless of today's outcome. You have shown Your love and faithfulness to us in the past and have promised it for our future, so our trust is in You. I give You great praise. Amen.

Surely, Lord, you bless the righteous; you surround them with your favor as with a shield.

PSALM 5:12

The Lord bestows favor and honor; no good thing does he withhold from those whose walk is blameless.

PSALM 84:11

FOR MY HUSBAND'S CHALLENGING JOB

Lord, my husband's job is physically demanding, often requiring him to be away on assignment. It is sometimes dangerous and dirty; he comes home exhausted and hungry. Thank You for giving him the necessary skills to work at this job and provide for his family. Please protect him and keep the enemy from distracting him or causing accidents. Surround him with helpful coworkers. Help me make his time at home with the children and me more comfortable and peaceful. Give me creative ideas for showing him how much I appreciate his hard work for us. May we find ways to have happy, relaxing times together when he is home. I'm so glad he knows You, Lord, and attends church with us when he is in town. Your blessings have been with us as a couple since we first fell in love. Thank You, Lord, for my faithful, hardworking man of God. Amen.

Let all who take refuge in you be glad; let them ever sing for joy. Spread your protection over them, that those who love your name may rejoice in you.

Psalm 5:11

O Lord our God, let your sweet beauty rest upon us and give us favor. Come work with us, and then our works will endure, and give us success in all we do.

Psalm 90:17 tpt

FOR MY UNSAVED HUSBAND

Heavenly Father, I grieve that my husband does not yet know You or grasp the depths of Your love for him. Help _____ [husband's name] fully accept that Jesus died for his sins and that he truly needs a Savior. Let him feel Your great love. Please send a godly man across his path to share Your truth in a way he can understand and receive. I pray he will recognize that the lies he has believed about You, and about what it means to be a Christian, are a deception of the enemy. Give him a desire to read the Bible and receive Your guidance in applying its principles to his life. Help me be a good, loving example to him. I declare that evil lying spirits can no longer blind him to truth. Lord, I give thanks that You will rescue and save him, in Jesus' name, Amen.

Open their eyes so that they may turn from darkness to light and from the dominion of Satan to God, that they may receive forgiveness of sins and an inheritance among those who have been sanctified by faith in Me.

ACTS 26:18 NASB

. . . with gentleness correcting those who are in opposition, if perhaps God may grant them repentance leading to the knowledge of the truth, and they may come to their senses and escape from the snare of the devil, having been held captive by him to do his will.

2 TIMOTHY 2:25–26 NASB

PRAYER TO STRENGTHEN OUR MARRIAGE

Lord, Your Word says that the thief comes to steal, kill and destroy, but that You came to give us life abundantly [see John 10:10]. I know the enemy tries to bring division between couples. This is his strategy to destroy marriages and break up families. Please, Father, help _____ [husband's name] and me find ways to strengthen our marriage. It is so easy for us to get caught up with the pressures of life and neglect praying together to seek Your wisdom. We need Your direction in mentoring our children and making important family decisions. Help us carve out quality time together to make our marriage stronger as we learn to communicate more clearly. Give us patience to hear each other out when a misunderstanding arises, rather than ignoring the issue. May we always honor one another and speak the truth in love. Faithful God, thank You for answering my prayer, Amen.

Therefore, as God's chosen people, holy and dearly loved, clothe yourselves with compassion, kindness, humility, gentleness and patience. Bear with each other and forgive one another if any of you has a grievance against someone. Forgive as the Lord forgave you.

Colossians 3:12–13

Wives, fit in with your husbands' plans; for then if they refuse to listen when you talk to them about the Lord, they will be won by your respectful, pure behavior. Your godly lives will speak to them better than any words. . . .

You husbands must be careful of your wives, being thoughtful of their needs and honoring them as the weaker sex. Remember that you and your wife are partners in receiving God's blessings, and if you don't treat her as you should, your prayers will not get ready answers.

1 Peter 3:1–2, 7 TLB

FOR ESTRANGED FAMILY MEMBERS

Father God, I pray that disputes among my family members that have kept them estranged for years can be settled, and relationships can be reconciled. In some cases, the standoff has gone on for so long that I'm not sure what the original grievance was about. I know the enemy strives to sow misunderstanding, conflict and division in families. But I stand on Your promise that You came to heal the brokenhearted and bind up their wounds [see Psalm 147:3]. Please intervene to heal this breach and restore the relationship between _____ and _____ [names]. No doubt there were accusations and angry words spoken on both sides, but reconciliation is possible. Holy Spirit, reveal to them the power of forgiveness to reestablish a bond of respect and acceptance. Give each party involved a desire to right the wrongs and restore peace. I pray this in the name of Jesus, our great Peacemaker, Amen.

Love is patient; love is kind. Love isn't envious, doesn't boast, brag, or strut about. There's no arrogance in love; it's never rude, crude, or indecent—it's not self-absorbed. Love isn't easily upset. Love doesn't tally wrongs or celebrate injustice; but truth—yes, truth—is love's delight!

1 Corinthians 13:4–6 voice

I urge you to live a life worthy of the calling you have received. Be completely humble and gentle; be patient, bearing with one another in love. Make every effort to keep the unity of the Spirit through the bond of peace.

Ephesians 4:1–3

FOR MY FRIENDS

Heavenly Father, thank You for the gift of friends. I especially appreciate my "keeper" friends who are only a phone call or text message away when I need prayer, encouragement, comfort or support. Bring the people of Your choice into my life at the right time, and help our relationships be what You desire them to be. Lord, I don't take lightly these special friendships. These "keepers" are women who not only pray for me and I for them, but we have trust and accountability for one another. Guard our friendships, and help me be a faithful friend. Send me a prayer alert when I need to stand in the gap on behalf of one of these women. Guide me so I do not choose wrong acquaintances. I'm so glad Jesus enjoyed His friendships on earth and gives us an encouraging example to follow. Amen.

Anxious fear brings depression, but a life-giving word of encouragement can do wonders to restore joy to the heart.

Lovers of God give good advice to their friends, but the counsel of the wicked will lead them astray.

PROVERBS 12:25–26 TPT

A dear friend will love you no matter what, and a family sticks together through all kinds of trouble.

PROVERBS 17:17 TPT

PRAYER TO MEND BROKEN RELATIONSHIPS

Lord, I have not tried hard enough to restore some broken relationships, and I need Your help. Yes, I have longtime friends whom I've forgiven. But we are not yet at the "mended" level that You or I desire. Help us listen to each other with open hearts and communicate with understanding and humility. Forgive my pride—always wanting to be right. Pleasing You is much more important. Lord, I trust You to open a door at the right time for me to reach out to _____ [friends' names], whether in person or via letter, email, phone or texting, to suggest we meet for lunch. Give me the right words to express my regret and my genuine desire for some level of our friendship to be restored. Thank You, Lord, for being our great Reconciler, Amen.

Do to others as you would have them to do to you. . . . Be merciful, just as your Father is merciful. Do not judge, and you will not be judged. Do not condemn, and you will not be condemned. Forgive, and you will be forgiven.

Luke 6:31, 36–37

Dear friend, do not imitate what is evil but what is good. Anyone who does what is good is from God. Anyone who does what is evil has not seen God.

3 John 1:11

PRAYER TO BLESS MY PARENTS

Father, I thank You for the parents You gave me. For their love and example of living a wholesome, good life. Help me honor them in the way You intended for children to honor their parents. Yes, there were times when they disappointed me. And I confess that I have failed them, too. Help us resolve any misunderstandings and quickly forgive each other, just as Christ forgives us. Please let Your love flow through us one to another, without enemy interference. Thank You for the talents I inherited through their DNA and for the encouragement they gave me through the years to develop my own abilities. Give them strength, wisdom and good health. Bless them, Lord, and thank You for the blessing they have been to me. I ask in Jesus' name, Amen.

The LORD bless you and keep you; the LORD make His face shine upon you, and be gracious to you; the LORD lift up His countenance upon you, and give you peace.

NUMBERS 6:24–26 NKJV

Honor your father and your mother, as the LORD your God has commanded you, so that you may live long and that it may go well with you in the land the LORD your God is giving you.

DEUTERONOMY 5:16

FORGIVING MY PARENTS

Lord, my parents wounded me deeply by their hurtful words and treatment. I realize now that had their focus been on You, our home life could have been much more peaceful. But they were living in a dark place, with no understanding of Your power to help, had they called on You. Father, I choose to forgive them, and I ask You to forgive them. Please set all of us free from the enemy's stronghold of alienation and bitterness. Forgive me for the things I have thought or said that were dishonoring to my parents and displeasing to You. May Your perfect will be done in our lives. Give me Your wisdom about when to reach out to them to reestablish communication. Please continue to heal my emotional wounds and mend this broken relationship. I receive Your forgiveness and thank You for the cleansing and healing that it brings, Amen.

Therefore I tell you, whatever you ask for in prayer, believe that you have received it, and it will be yours. And when you stand praying, if you hold anything against anyone, forgive them, so that your Father in heaven may forgive you your sins.

MARK 11:24–26

When you forgive this man, I [Paul] forgive him, too. And when I forgive whatever needs to be forgiven, I do so with Christ's authority for your benefit, so that Satan will not outsmart us. For we are familiar with his evil schemes.

2 CORINTHIANS 2:10–12 NLT

(Note: You also can add the names of family members, friends or others you need to forgive. It is critically important that you not allow unforgiveness to hinder your walk with the Lord and your witness for Him.)

FOR MY AGING PARENT

Lord, my aging dad needs to make a change soon. Should we get him more help at home? Move him into an assisted living facility? Invite him to come live with me, far from his friends and familiar surroundings? We need Your wisdom to choose an affordable place where he can be happy and safe, and can make new friends. As his health begins to falter, please give him courage and hope. Keep the enemy of fear from tormenting his mind. Be his Comforter, Healer, Helper. Lord, help me shower him with the love and support he needs in these latter years of his life. I truly want what is best for his wellbeing. Thank You for the years he has been there for me. I'm trusting You for a few more, Amen.

He will not let your foot slip—he who watches over you will not slumber. . . .

The Lord will keep you from all harm—he will watch over your life.

Psalm 121:3, 7

But the wisdom that comes from heaven is first of all pure; then peace-loving, considerate, submissive, full of mercy and good fruit, impartial and sincere. Peacemakers who sow in peace reap a harvest of righteousness.

James 3:17–18

FOR A PARENT WITH DEMENTIA

Lord, I don't know my mother anymore. She has had such a decline in her mental ability, severe enough to interfere with her daily life. Gradually, dementia has caused problems with her memory, thinking and behavior. The state revoked her driver's license, so she is homebound, dependent on friends or taxis. She refuses to move into a senior residency or in with one of us adult children. She is stubborn, unreasonable and extremely angry with us for trying to offer her advice. This is not just an old-age symptom, but shows serious dementia. Show us how to deal with her situation and keep her safe. Lord, we need a solution. Please guide us to a doctor or social worker who can convince her of what is best for her remaining years. I love her dearly and am saddened by her regression. Please, God, move on her behalf. Help her. Help my siblings and me, Amen.

Surely He has borne our griefs and carried our sorrows; yet we esteemed Him stricken, smitten by God, and afflicted. But He was wounded for our transgressions, He was bruised for our iniquities; the chastisement for our peace was upon Him, and by His stripes we are healed.

Isaiah 53:4–5 nkjv

And thus He fulfilled what was spoken by the prophet Isaiah, He Himself took [in order to carry away] our weaknesses and infirmities and bore away our diseases.

Matthew 8:17 ampc

OVERALL DAILY PRAYER FOR FAMILY

*L*ord, I pray today for my family members[1] to experience Your

- Presence (Psalm 16:11; 31:20)
- Protection (Psalm 5:11; 72:12–14)
- Provision (Psalm 106:4–5; Philippians 4:19)
- Peace (Psalm 4:8; 29:11)
- Precious promises to be fulfilled (2 Corinthians 1:20; 2 Peter 1:4)

---

1. This prayer is excerpted in part from our book *A Woman's Guide to Spiritual Warfare* (Chosen, 2017), 224.

And then, Lord, for them to

- Acknowledge and praise You as their Savior and Giver of life
- Have discernment and wisdom, and not be deceived in decisions facing them
- Make wise choices financially and morally
- Find favor in the workplace and marketplace
- Cast their cares, worries and anxieties on You, trusting in You
- Have the right people come into their lives at the right time to fulfill Your plan for them
- Have a positive influence as they use their talents and skills to help others
- Experience Your healing and comforting touch
- Be on guard against participating in ungodly or illegal activities

Declaration

I declare that my family will serve God and fulfill His destiny for each of us. We will not fall into the traps of the enemy and be sidelined. As I intercede for my family and friends, I beseech God on their behalf, but I also stand boldly in spiritual battle between them and invisible enemy forces attempting to thwart their destiny. Because Jesus gave us authority over the enemy by the power of His shed blood, I decree that antichrist spirits and generational curses working with evil intent against my family will not prevail. I speak confusion to the ranks of the enemy, and I declare that no weapon formed against God's purposes for my family shall prosper, but shall instead be condemned [see Isaiah 54:17 NKJV]. As I lift up worship and praise to His holy name, I thank God that victory is the heritage of His people!

PART 6

Praying WHEN SINGLE

THANK YOU FOR MY FRIENDS

Lord, thank You for my extra-special friends. I cherish our relationships. These people give me spiritual inspiration, hope and courage. They are there when I need to laugh and when I need to cry. Some are more studious, while others are great fun pals. But I appreciate and pray for all of them. They believe in me and trust me. Most of the time they understand me, but even if they don't, they will listen without condemning me. Yet I want to be open to hear their perspective and logic. May I be to them what they are to me—their confidante and a trustworthy companion. Lord, I'm grateful that they love and follow You, too, as we hold one another morally and ethically accountable for our choices. Help us recognize and foil the enemy's attacks together. Thank You for each of these genuine treasures in my life. Bless them abundantly, Amen.

Perfume and incense bring joy to the heart, and the pleasantness of a friend springs from their heartfelt advice.

 Do not forsake your friend.

PROVERBS 27:9–10

Two are better than one. . . . If either of them falls down, one can help the other up. But pity anyone who falls and has no one to help them up. . . . Though one may be overpowered, two can defend themselves. A cord of three strands is not quickly broken.

ECCLESIASTES 4:9–10, 12

IT'S NOT EASY BEING SINGLE

Father God, I'm content with my life as a single woman, though it's not always easy. I'm lonely occasionally, and I do have secret desires. Sometimes I fight sexual feelings if I watch certain movies or TV shows, or read suggestive romance novels. Lord, You know my heart and my thoughts. Please help me be the woman of God You want me to be, and help me fulfill Your purpose for my life. If marriage is in Your plan for me, then I trust You to bring the right man across my path. Help me embrace this season of single life with enthusiasm, not regret or remorse. Thank You for my job, plus great friends who are there when I need them most. Strengthen me in the days ahead to avoid any enemy pitfalls that would throw me offtrack from Your plan. Help me remain sensitive to the Holy Spirit's leading, in Jesus' name, Amen.

An unmarried woman or virgin is concerned about the Lord's affairs: Her aim is to be devoted to the Lord in both body and spirit. But a married woman is concerned about the affairs of this world—how she can please her husband.

1 Corinthians 7:34

. . . being confident of this, that he who began a good work in you will carry it on to completion until the day of Christ Jesus.

Philippians 1:6

REACHING OUT TO OTHERS

*L*ord, forgive me for focusing so much on my own problems and interests, and for sometimes failing to reach out to those around me. I choose today to release my own needs into Your loving hands. Help me be a blessing to others as the Holy Spirit pours Your love through me. Begin to open doors connecting me with people and places where You want me to become involved in my community. Also, please open a door for me to go on a missions trip. I want to enlarge my vision using the skills You've given me to make a difference in the lives of others. Thank You for leading me, and for protecting me from enemy interference along the way. Give me wisdom, understanding and favor as I launch into this pursuit to reach out beyond my comfort zone. Thank You that You will be with me as I go, Amen.

To them God has chosen to make known among the Gentiles the glorious riches of this mystery, which is Christ in you, the hope of glory. He is the one we proclaim, admonishing and teaching everyone with all wisdom, so that we may present everyone fully mature in Christ.

Colossians 1:27–28

What you heard from me, keep as the pattern of sound teaching, with faith and love in Christ Jesus. Guard the good deposit that was entrusted to you— guard it with the help of the Holy Spirit who lives in us.

2 Timothy 1:13–14

THANK YOU FOR MY FAMILY

Lord, I thank You for my life right now. While I live alone, I'm not lonesome. I have a wonderful extended family. Thank You for my parents, brothers, sisters, cousins and assorted aunts and uncles. Though my siblings are married, they've made a place for me in their families. When we can't visit in person, we keep up through phone calls and social media. I enjoy every opportunity to shower my love on nieces and nephews, especially for their birthday celebrations and other special occasions. Thank You for the happy memories we're making. Help our family continue to enjoy close relationships and not allow the enemy to bring division among us. I'm grateful to have such a loving, special family. Please remind me to be faithful to pray for them when special needs arise. Bless them each and every one, Amen.

Therefore, as we have opportunity, let us do good to all people, especially to those who belong to the family of believers.

GALATIANS 6:10

May God be gracious to us and bless us and make his face shine on us.

PSALM 67:1

AFTER A BROKEN RELATIONSHIP

Lord, please heal me from the pain of this breakup. I loved and trusted him and expected to be married soon. How could I have been so blind to the indicators of trouble ahead? Thank You for waking me up to his true nature and strengthening me to break it off. I feel so violated. God, help me overcome grief, self-pity, humiliation, rejection, shame and anger. I renounce the enemy's effort to keep me in bondage to these negative emotions. Help me see myself as You see me—a beloved daughter. I am looking forward to Your better plan for my life. Thank You for sparing me from marrying the wrong man. Enable me to forgive him and move on with my recovery. Please give me keen discernment about any future relationships. Thank You for loving me with unconditional love and being my anchor of hope. I love You back, Amen.

Let all that I am wait quietly before God, for my hope is in him. He alone is my rock and my salvation, my fortress where I will not be shaken. My victory and honor come from God alone. He is my refuge, a rock where no enemy can reach me.

Psalm 62:5–7 NLT

Life will be brighter than noonday, and darkness will become like morning. You will be secure, because there is hope; you will look about you and take your rest in safety.

Job 11:17–18

A NEW RELATIONSHIP

*D*ear God, there is a special man in my life right now. I need Your help to keep our friendship what You want it to be—no more and no less. I don't know whether what I feel for him is real love or just infatuation springing out of my deep longing for a meaningful relationship. And I'm not at all sure what his intentions are toward me. Please keep me from reading into his actions a deeper interest than what he really feels. Father, protect me from being deceived and following the enemy's distraction down a wrong path. Please reveal Your will to me. Don't let me miss Your best; following Your will is my highest priority. Help me guard my heart and not pursue a relationship that doesn't have Your blessing. I ask this in the name of my Savior, Jesus Christ, Amen.

The LORD says, "I will guide you along the best pathway for your life. I will advise you and watch over you...."

Many sorrows come to the wicked, but unfailing love surrounds those who trust the LORD. So rejoice in the LORD and be glad, all you who obey him! Shout for joy, all you whose hearts are pure!

PSALM 32:8, 10–11 NLT

Guard your heart above all else, for it determines the course of your life.

PROVERBS 4:23 NLT

SINGLE AFTER A DIVORCE

O Lord, help! I'm a "divorcée." How I hate that label. Since my marriage vows are broken, I feel betrayed, angry, fearful. And worried about all the decisions facing me. Yes, the enemy comes to destroy relationships. But also to harass me with a sense of hopelessness, fear of the unknown, doubt, unbelief and loneliness. Please give me the strength to forgive _____ [ex-husband's name] for his actions that led to this divorce. Also, help me forgive the friends who abandoned me. Lord, I give You my guilt, anger, disappointment and sense of failure. I refuse to be intimidated by the enemy's schemes any longer. I trust You, Father, to meet my every need—especially for financial security and suitable housing. Thank You for forgiving me and giving me a new, clean start. May the Holy Spirit comfort me, restore hope in my self-worth, and give assurance of Your guidance for the future, Amen.

*As for God, his way is perfect: The L*ORD*'s word is flawless; he shields all who take refuge in him. For who is God besides the L*ORD*? And who is the Rock except our God? It is God who arms me with strength and keeps my way secure.*

PSALM 18:30–32

*"For the L*ORD *has called you like a woman forsaken and grieved in spirit, like a youthful wife when you were refused," says your God. " . . . but with everlasting kindness I will have mercy on you," says the L*ORD*, your Redeemer.*

ISAIAH 54:6, 8 NKJV

SINGLE AGAIN AS A WIDOW

*L*ord, I'm sad for my loss, but grateful that my husband is now in heaven with You after _____ [his heart attack, his car crash, suffering with . . .]. Please help me adjust to this new state of widowhood. Some call it the sorority no woman wants to join. Enable me to make wise choices in managing the funds I have to live on. Decisions seem overwhelming—disposing of property if necessary, finding a job, finding a place to live and planning for an uncertain future. As You guide me through the grieving process, I choose to believe that You will work for my good, giving me favor and divine appointments in the days ahead. Protect me from the evil one at this vulnerable season of my life. Help me stay connected with friends and prayer partners. Thank You, Father, that You are healing me of sadness and will start to reveal the path You have for me— beginning now, Amen.

You lead me with your secret wisdom. And following you brings me into your brightness and glory! Whom have I in heaven but you? You're all I want! No one on earth means as much to me as you. Lord, . . . when I trust in you, I have a strong and glorious presence protecting and anointing me. Forever you're all I need!

Psalm 73:24–26 TPT

He has sent me to bind up the brokenhearted, to proclaim freedom for the captives and release from darkness for the prisoners, to proclaim the year of the Lord's favor . . . to comfort all who mourn . . . to bestow on them a crown of beauty instead of ashes, the oil of joy instead of mourning, and a garment of praise instead of a spirit of despair.

Isaiah 61:1–3

Declaration

I decree that I will be the woman of God He created me to be, content with this season of my life. I will use my experience and skills to help others and find more ways to serve Him, my extended family and my community. Believing that God knows the people with whom He wants me connected and the places He wants me to be, I will remain open for His direction. When the enemy tries to sabotage God's plan for me, I will wield my spiritual weapons to overcome the evil one [see Ephesians 6:10–17]. In today's ever-changing culture, I depend on God to impart His wisdom, understanding and favor so I can make a positive impact on those in my sphere of influence. I declare that Father God will protect me and provide the finances I need so I can accomplish His purposes.

PART 7

Praying through TOUGH TIMES

DEALING WITH TRAUMA

*L*ord, my mind is bombarded with questions about the trauma in my life right now. Nothing seems to make sense. Trying to think through various solutions only adds to my frustration. I realize that finding answers that satisfy may not be possible. But Lord, I'm asking You to give me Your direction and comfort in the midst of this turmoil. Your Word assures me that I can give my burdens to You because You care about what happens to my loved ones and me. Help me hand over to You all my questions, and please silence the enemy's voice that seeks to assault my mind with condemnation. I choose to trust Your faithfulness, no matter what happens. And I pray that I will emerge from this attack wiser and more Christlike. I praise You in advance for the victory that's coming, Amen.

The Lord your God in your midst, the Mighty One, will save; He will rejoice over you with gladness, He will quiet you with His love, He will rejoice over you with singing.

Zephaniah 3:17 nkjv

Humble yourselves, therefore, under God's mighty hand, that he may lift you up in due time. Cast all your anxiety on him because he cares for you.

1 Peter 5:6–7

HELP ME GET THROUGH THE DAY

Heavenly Father, help me get through this day. You know that a tough and difficult day faces me. Please give me wisdom and strength, and give me favor with those I'll be interacting with. I also need some encouragement. God, I believe Your grace is sufficient for whatever comes my way. You alone know how my day will turn out, but I trust You to guide me through it. I stand on Your Word, which declares that when the enemy comes in like a flood, Your Spirit will lift up a standard against him [see Isaiah 59:19 NKJV]. So, as grim situations and challenges attempt to overwhelm me, I trust You to raise up a standard on my behalf. With Your promises in my heart and Your constant angelic help, I begin this new day praising You, my loving Standard-Bearer. In Jesus' name, Amen.

May he give you the desire of your heart and make all your plans succeed. May we shout for joy over your victory and lift up our banners in the name of our God.

Psalm 20:4–5

For the Lord gives wisdom; from his mouth come knowledge and understanding. He holds success in store for the upright, he is a shield to those whose walk is blameless, for he guards the course of the just and protects the way of his faithful ones.

Proverbs 2:6–8

FALSELY ACCUSED

Lord Jesus, You know that I was falsely accused. I didn't do what the gossip mill says. Because You have given us authority over the enemy through the power of Your name, I stand against this attack on my character and reputation. I now declare that any malicious words—whether spoken, written or prayed—are rendered null and void by the blood You shed for us. Tongues of accusers must be silent. Thank You, Lord, that truth will prevail, while false and hateful words will fall to the ground. I trust You to defend me from gossip and devious actions on the part of _____ [bosses, jealous co-workers, neighbors, betraying friends, etc.] and vindicate me before my enemies in due time. May the accusers see the error of their ways and turn to You with repentant hearts. Lord, You are my Refuge, my Defender, my Savior and my Redeemer. How I praise You! Amen.

Contend, O Lord, with those who contend with me; fight against those who fight against me. Take hold of buckler and shield and rise up for my help. . . . For without cause they hid their net for me; without cause they dug a pit for my soul. . . .

Let them shout for joy and rejoice, who favor my vindication; and let them say continually, "The Lord be magnified."

Psalm 35:1–2, 7, 27 nasb

Be still before the Lord and wait patiently for him; do not fret when people succeed in their ways, when they carry out their wicked schemes.

Refrain from anger and turn from wrath; do not fret—it leads only to evil.

Psalm 37:7–8

OVERCOMING DISAPPOINTMENT

Lord God, I am struggling with big disappointment in the people who let me down. And frustration because my expectations didn't materialize. When I prayed about the situation, I felt certain that the outcome would be positive. But maybe I was motivated by my own desires. Now I need Your grace to deal with the fallout. Lord, please help me forgive the ones who disappointed me, so I can get through this without bitterness. I say *no* to the enemy, who keeps harassing me over this upset. And I refuse to listen to the accusing voices trying to speak to me. I choose to believe that You, Father, have better things for my future—greater than I can comprehend. Help me through the waiting period until I see Your answer. Thank You for sending Jesus to be my Rescuer and Savior, Amen.

"My thoughts are nothing like your thoughts," says the Lord. "And my ways are far beyond anything you could imagine. For just as the heavens are higher than the earth, so my ways are higher than your ways and my thoughts higher than your thoughts."

Isaiah 55:8–9 NLT

But as it is written: "Eye has not seen, nor ear heard, nor have entered into the heart of man the things which God has prepared for those who love Him."

1 Corinthians 2:9 NKJV

LORD, I NEED FINANCES

*L*ord, financial setbacks are attempting to lure me into a panic. I tell the enemy to get off, get out, get away from our family's finances and no longer steal or withhold what is rightfully ours in Jesus' name. We are needing to pay unexpectedly for _____ [higher taxes, higher cost of living, expensive auto or equipment repairs]. Father, I war to have the enemy release the resources that You want us to have for completing the work You desire for us to accomplish. Help us be obedient to You in giving tithes and offerings for the work of the Kingdom, despite these attacks. I call in the necessary funds to come without delay. I pray protection over our home and all our possessions. Thank You, heavenly Father, for Your promises that You will provide all our needs. I give You great praise, Amen.

Remember the Eternal One your God. He's the One who gives you the power to get wealth, so He can keep the covenant promises He made to your ancestors, as He is doing now.

>> Deuteronomy 8:18 voice

And God is able to bless you abundantly, so that in all things at all times, having all that you need, you will abound in every good work.

>> 2 Corinthians 9:8

LORD, I NEED A JOB

Father, I need a job. Really soon. You know my desperate situation, my needs and the circumstances that brought me to this place. And You know my skills and available work hours. Please guide me to the right people who can give me leads or recommend me for job openings they know about. Give me favor to land the best position "fit" for my experience—one that will provide an adequate salary to cover my living expenses. I promise to serve my boss with integrity and faithfulness, be a team player and work for the betterment of the company. Lord, I want to please You in everything I do and say in the workplace. I now trust You to direct me to the right job and keep the enemy from interfering. Help me always be a good employee and a faithful witness for You, Amen.

Whatever you do, work at it with all your heart, as working for the Lord, not for human masters, since you know that you will receive an inheritance from the Lord as a reward. It is the Lord Christ you are serving.

Colossians 3:23–24

And my God will meet all your needs according to the riches of his glory in Christ Jesus.

Philippians 4:19

LORD, I NEED HEALING

*L*ord, based on recent lab results, my doctor has diagnosed me with _____ [name the illness]. I hold tightly to my faith, knowing that with You, I can beat this. Jesus, You not only healed the sick while on earth; You also gave Your disciples authority to heal sickness and disease [see Matthew 10:1]. So healing is available to me today. I know You can heal me miraculously, or through doctors and medical technology. Guide me in choosing the best treatment. Provide people of faith to stand with me in prayer and spiritual warfare against this evil thing that has attacked my body. Also help me make lifestyle changes to improve my health. Give my family and me the courage, strength, comfort and hope we need as we look forward to my recovery. I stand on Your Word that with You nothing is impossible [see Matthew 19:26]. I praise You, my Lord and Healer, Amen.

Surely He has borne our griefs and carried our sorrows; yet we esteemed Him stricken, smitten by God, and afflicted. But He was wounded for our transgressions, He was bruised for our iniquities; the chastisement for our peace was upon Him, and by His stripes we are healed.

ISAIAH 53:4–5 NKJV

Stretch out your hand to heal and perform signs and wonders through the name of your holy servant Jesus.

ACTS 4:30

TRADING SELF-PITY FOR HOPE

Lord, I'm drowning in self-pity, rehashing all the reasons I've lost my hope. Obstacles seem impossible to overcome, and it seems my personal dreams have been dashed. All I can focus on is me, myself and I. Instead, I need to concentrate on You, heavenly Father! You are the one who is for me, not against me. You can reverse my trouble. I know the battleground is in my mind. So I choose now to resist the voice of the enemy and bring my thoughts and words into agreement with Your Word. Lord, I give You my self-pity, misery, defeatism. I gladly exchange them for Your hope, and I take refuge under the shadow of Your wings. Lord, please help me and hold my hand as I walk it out, Amen.

Show me the wonders of your great love, you who save by your right hand those who take refuge in you from their foes. Keep me as the apple of your eye; hide me in the shadow of your wings.

PSALM 17:7–8

Stay alert! Watch out for your great enemy, the devil. He prowls around like a roaring lion, looking for someone to devour. Stand firm against him, and be strong in your faith. Remember that your family of believers all over the world is going through the same kind of suffering you are.

1 PETER 5:8–9 NLT

DEATH OF A LOVED ONE

*L*ord, my mom has died. When I got the news, I felt numb as my knees buckled, and I began shaking with deep sobs. During my recent visit there, it seemed to her caregivers and me that she was improving, so I returned home. My mom, my dearest friend—I will never hear her voice again or feel her encouraging hugs. Lord, please come in the midst of my pain and heal my deep grief. I do rejoice that Jesus was her Savior and that she is now in heaven, beyond suffering. Help us plan a service that will honor her life and her years of faithful service to You. Thank You for all the things she taught me and the way she modeled motherhood in such a sweet, simple way. Thank You for my special mom. I'm trusting You to be with me in the practical things I must do now, Amen.

She watches over the affairs of her household and does not eat the bread of idleness. Her children arise and call her blessed; her husband also, and he praises her: "Many women do noble things, but you surpass them all."

Proverbs 31:27–29

Praise be to the God and Father of our Lord Jesus Christ, the Father of compassion and the God of all comfort, who comforts us in all our troubles, so that we can comfort those in any trouble with the comfort we ourselves receive from God.

2 Corinthians 1:3–4

Declaration

I declare that my faithful God will see me through these tough times! When I feel weary, worn down with burdens, broken and hopeless, I will watch expectantly for the God of my salvation. He will hear me. And though I fall, I will rise. Even if I dwell in darkness, the Lord is a light for me [see Micah 7:7–8 NASB]. When I cry to my faithful Father, He quiets my storm. He relieves my distress. I place my hope, faith and trust in Him, for my Lord is good and His love endures forever. The blood of Jesus covers my family and me, and that blood deflects every fiery dart the enemy directs toward us. I proclaim with the psalmist,

> There is only one strong, safe, and secure place for me; it's in God alone and I love him! He's the one who gives me strength and skill for the battle. He's my shelter of love and my fortress of faith, who wraps himself around me as a secure shield. I hide myself in this one who subdues enemies before me.
>
> PSALM 144:1–2 TPT

PART 8

Praying in MY SENIOR YEARS

MY SENIOR YEARS

Heavenly Father, please help me adjust to this new age bracket I've now advanced into. Though I have dreaded this milestone, I really want to walk through my latter years gracefully, adjusting and transitioning well. I place high expectations on the something new You want me to experience. Increase my strength, and help me not to miss Your better plan for my senior years as You reveal it to me. I resist the enemy's attempt to isolate me and keep me from fulfilling Your purposes for me in this season. Holy Spirit, teach me and guide me as I begin this unfamiliar journey. Thank You, Lord, for every year You have graciously given me. I pray in the name of my Savior, Jesus, Amen.

Even when I am old and gray, do not forsake me, O God, till I declare your power to the next generation, your mighty acts to all who are to come.

Psalm 71:18

Even to your old age and gray hairs I am he, I am he who will sustain you. I have made you and I will carry you; I will sustain you and I will rescue you.

Isaiah 46:4

LORD, I'M LONELY!

Father God, I never imagined that I would feel so lonely when I grew older. I long for a get-together, a shared meal, coffee with friends. I need assurance that I am wanted, needed, appreciated. Surely others my age also need a touch, a hug or a pat on the back now and then. Help me be more willing to invite others to my place for fellowship. Thank You, God, that the enemy is defeated and has no authority to harass me in this season of my life. Help me shift the focus off myself and find ways to show Your compassion to other lonely ones. May I never forget that You are always with me, even in my loneliest hours. I want my home to be a sanctuary where Your presence always abides and where those who visit can receive Your peace. I pray in Jesus' name, Amen.

Turn to me and be gracious to me, for I am lonely and afflicted. Relieve the troubles of my heart and free me from my anguish. Look on my affliction and my distress.

PSALM 25:16–18

Be filled with the Spirit, speaking to one another in psalms and hymns and spiritual songs, singing and making melody in your heart to the Lord, giving thanks always for all things to God the Father in the name of our Lord Jesus Christ.

EPHESIANS 5:18–20 NKJV

HELP ME MAKE NEW FRIENDS

Lord, as I've advanced in years and have become less active, I realize that I need to find new friends. Several have died or moved away, so my circle of close acquaintances has been shrinking. Father, strengthen me to shake off complacency, reach out to others and be more outgoing toward those You send across my path. Help me find a suitable Bible study or prayer group that I could join. Or show me whether I should consider opening my home for a few women to gather here for prayer, fellowship and sharing meals together. I resist sinking into isolation, as I know that's a trap of the enemy. Lord, I trust You will provide guidance to help me find new friends in the days ahead. I give You thanks and praise in advance for answering my prayer, in Jesus' name, Amen.

Anxiety weighs down the heart, but a kind word cheers it up.

The righteous choose their friends carefully, but the way of the wicked leads them astray.

Proverbs 12:25–26

One who has unreliable friends soon comes to ruin, but there is a friend who sticks closer than a brother.

Proverbs 18:24

HERE AM I; USE ME

Lord, we seniors have a wealth of wisdom, knowledge and experience we could share with younger women. Our talent and skills for certain tasks should not be wasted just because we are older. Open the door to opportunities for me to help others succeed in their callings. If there are younger women You want me to mentor, please bring them my way and help us connect our generations. I want to be an encourager, a prayer partner, a teacher to impart something positive into a few women coming behind me. I refuse the enemy's interference in Your chosen plan for our meeting together and mutually learning from one another. Thank You, Lord, for the ways You will cause our sharing with each other to happen. May I be vigilant to share more about Your love and Your desire to equip us to do Your will, Amen.

Therefore encourage one another and build each other up, just as in fact you are doing.

1 Thessalonians 5:11

Each of you should use whatever gift you have received to serve others, as faithful stewards of God's grace in its various forms. If anyone speaks, they should do so as one who speaks the very words of God. If anyone serves, they should do so with the strength God provides, so that in all things God may be praised through Jesus Christ.

1 Peter 4:10–11

I NEED LEGAL HELP

Lord, I need good legal advice. Please help me choose dependable, honorable counsel. Protect me from being deceived or taken advantage of by dishonest lawyers. Help me hire the attorney who will best represent my cause in this court case. Give him/her wisdom and a strategy for how to resolve the issues I am facing. I choose not to be intimidated by those trying to steal what I'm entitled to have. Lord, I never expected to be in a legal dispute like this, and I desperately need Your help in fighting this battle. Thank You for Your watchfulness over me and my household. Thank You that justice will prevail. I love You and trust You, Lord, Amen.

O Lord, You are the portion of my inheritance and my cup; You maintain my lot. The lines have fallen to me in pleasant places; yes, I have a good inheritance.

I will bless the Lord who has given me counsel; my heart also instructs me in the night seasons. I have set the Lord always before me; because He is at my right hand I shall not be moved.

Psalm 16:5–8 nkjv

I have chosen the way of faithfulness; I have set my heart on your laws. I hold fast to your statutes, Lord; do not let me be put to shame.

Psalm 119:30–31

PRAYING WHEN A SHUT-IN

*L*ord, confinement to a wheelchair has altered my lifestyle. Suddenly I've lost my independence. I often forget I can't walk across the room to pick up something. Or drive a car to the grocery store. Or survive without someone to help me with ordinary tasks. My only exercise is when the physical therapist helps me stretch some muscles and take a few steps with a walker. Help me not to overeat, lest I gain weight. Help me not to become addicted to watching TV shows or reading books that prevent me from keeping a positive attitude. I refuse the enemy's attempt to draw me into hopelessness. Thank You, Lord, that I've gained a deeper fellowship with You, spending more time praying for people and nations. I'm grateful for the quiet times alone when I can pray and worship aloud. I praise You for being my Hope, my Refuge, my Redeemer, Amen.

Then they cried to the LORD in their trouble, and he saved them from their distress. He brought them out of darkness, the utter darkness, and broke away their chains. Let them give thanks to the LORD for his unfailing love.

PSALM 107:13–15

Defend my cause and redeem me; preserve my life according to your promise.

PSALM 119:154

HOPE FOR WIDOWS

Lord, this transition into widowhood as a senior is somewhat terrifying. Since my husband's death, I've been on a roller coaster of emotional ups and downs. Grief. Guilt. Anxiety. Loneliness. Money worries. Wading through piles of paperwork. Life-changing decisions. I need a place of safety and the right location for my future. Do I move? How do I downsize? Please give me wisdom and put trustworthy people in my life to advise me in making practical decisions. I know You have a plan for my latter years, so I trust You to begin showing me how to function in this new season of widowhood. When I feel overwhelmed with discouragement and despair, remind me to recall and declare Scriptures of hope to push back the enemy's attack. Lord, I thank You in advance, for You are now my Husband. I trust You to see me through, Amen.

The widow who is really in need and left all alone puts her hope in God and continues night and day to pray and to ask God for help.

1 Timothy 5:5

You will . . . remember no more the reproach of your widowhood. For your Maker is your husband—the Lord Almighty is his name—the Holy One of Israel is your Redeemer; he is called the God of all the earth.

Isaiah 54:4–5

LEAVING A LEGACY OF PRAYER

*L*ord, prayer has been my lifeline. Thank You that I am free to talk to You night or day. We've had some wonderful conversations as I've prayed about family, friends, finances and many other things. I've seen warfare prayers bring change to people's hearts and lives, and even unbelievers were sometimes touched. I've watched prayer send confusion into the enemy's camp by Your miracle-working power. Lord, my desire is to leave a legacy of prayer—that people I've prayed for and with will continue with prayer quests on their own. May the prayers I've planted for the future be answered in Your timing in the lives of loved ones, friends and leaders, even if I'm not around to see it when it happens. I give You honor, glory and praise for every answered prayer! Amen.

I am always thankful to my God as I remember you in my prayers because I'm hearing reports about your faith in the Lord Jesus and how much love you have for all his holy followers. I pray for you that the faith we share may effectively deepen your understanding of every good thing that belongs to you in Christ.

Philemon 4–6 tpt

He [an angel] was given much incense to offer, with the prayers of all God's people, on the golden altar in front of the throne. The smoke of the incense, together with the prayers of God's people, went up before God from the angel's hand.

Revelation 8:3–4

MY REMEMBRANCES

*L*ord, looking back over my life, I cherish so many memories of people, experiences and places that deeply inspired and impacted me. I want to write about the most significant ones for my great-grandchildren, yet unborn. May they understand, even after I'm gone, how greatly You displayed Your love and power in my life. While writing "My Remembrances," help me recall the special people and occasions I need to include. Also, I don't want to neglect mentioning the times You intervened when the enemy tried to abort Your purpose for me. I pray that when my descendants read my memoir, they will have a desire to follow You, especially if they've not yet committed their lives to You. Thank You for all the happy moments that gave me such happy memories. And especially for the wonderful people I encountered along the way, Amen.

We will tell the next generation the praiseworthy deeds of the LORD, his power, and the wonders he has done. He decreed statutes for Jacob and established the law in Israel, which he commanded our ancestors to teach their children, so the next generation would know them, even the children yet to be born, and they in turn would tell their children. Then they would put their trust in God and would not forget his deeds but would keep his commands.

PSALM 78:4–7

Then Job replied to the LORD:
"I know you can do all things; no purpose of yours can be thwarted."

JOB 42:1–2

FIGHT THE GOOD FIGHT

Heavenly Father, at the end my life's journey, I yearn to know it can be said that I fought the good fight. I kept the faith. I finished my race well, fulfilling Your purpose for me. I pray that my life influenced people for good, not bad, and was pleasing to You in all its aspects. Thank You, Father, for forgiving my sin and transferring me from the dominion of darkness to the Kingdom of Your Son [see Colossians 1:13]. Thank You for the wonderful life I've had serving an extraordinary God and being blessed with family and friends. Because I've embraced Jesus as my Savior, I know You have a place prepared for me in heaven. I trust that when I'm welcomed home, I can hear You say, "Well done, good and faithful servant." Jesus, thank You for dying for me and giving me the privilege to represent You in the earth, Amen.

Let not your heart be troubled; you believe in God, believe also in Me. In My Father's house are many mansions; if it were not so, I would have told you. I go to prepare a place for you. And if I go and prepare a place for you, I will come again and receive you to Myself; that where I am, there you may be also.

JOHN 14:1–3 NKJV

I have fought the good fight, I have finished the race, I have kept the faith. Now there is in store for me the crown of righteousness, which the Lord, the righteous Judge, will award to me on that day—and not only to me, but also to all who have longed for his appearing.

2 TIMOTHY 4:7–8

PRAISING GOD IN MY GOLDEN YEARS

My loving Father, I remain Your thankful daughter. You have brought me through trials and tribulations. Through happy times and sad ones. Through disappointments and awesome times of unexpected blessings. You have wrapped Your arms about me. Whispered encouragement and hope to my sometimes hopeless heart. And always, always You have been there when I yelled, "Help!" or shouted, "Thank You!" You are my very present help in trouble. You rescue me when demonic voices try to make me want to throw in the towel. You are my Prayer Answerer, Rescuer and faithful Provider. I praise You for who You are and for what You have done *for* me and *with* me. I look forward to some wonderful golden years ahead in which I will keep loving, serving and worshiping You. From Your faithful daughter, _____ [your name].

Lord, you are my God; I will exalt you and praise your name, for in perfect faithfulness you have done wonderful things, things planned long ago.

Isaiah 25:1

Great and marvelous are your deeds, Lord God Almighty. Just and true are your ways, King of the nations. Who will not fear you, Lord, and bring glory to your name? For you alone are holy. All nations will come and worship before you, for your righteous acts have been revealed.

Revelation 15:3–4

Declaration

I declare that with God's help, I am transitioning well into my latter season of life. I will not give in to despair and isolation. I will fight the good fight, keep the faith and finish my race well. Loneliness will no longer keep me focused on my own needs; I am determined to begin reaching out to others. I will be available to mentor and encourage younger women, sharing from some of my own experiences in both practical and spiritual ways. I declare that I will spend more time communicating with my heavenly Father and praying more fervently for my family, friends and nation. I give great thanks that Jesus has prepared a place for me when He calls me to leave this earth. With joy, I look forward to spending eternity with Him and with those who have gone on before me. I rejoice that my citizenship is in heaven!

PART 9

Praying FOR MY COMMUNITY & NATION

PRAYER FOR MY PASTOR AND CHURCH

*L*ord, thank You for my church and the senior pastor who faithfully serves us. Guide him as he teaches Your truth and equips us to reach out to those needing Your love. I pray blessings over him, and over his family, too; please protect them spiritually, physically and emotionally. Lord, give Pastor _____ [pastor's name] favor with local leaders, and courage to speak up for godly values both in the pulpit and in our community. Make him an influencer who can bring unity among the pastors of our area. In the name of Jesus, I stand against any spirit of disunity the enemy seeks to use to stir up division in our congregation. May we be willing to volunteer to serve in areas where help is needed, so we can more effectively impact our community. Help us walk in love toward our leaders and toward one another. I give You thanks, Amen.

So Christ himself gave the apostles, the prophets, the evangelists, the pastors and teachers, to equip his people for works of service, so that the body of Christ may be built up.

Ephesians 4:11–12

Let us hold fast the confession of our hope without wavering, for He who promised is faithful. And let us consider one another in order to stir up love and good works, not forsaking the assembling of ourselves together, as is the manner of some, but exhorting one another, and so much the more as you see the Day approaching.

Hebrews 10:23–25 NKJV

CORPORATE PRAYER FOR MY COUNTRY

Lord, help our local churches stand together as one "prayer force" in intercession for our nation. Though we may have doctrinal differences, the Church, the Body of Christ, is Your representative on earth. Help us address issues that are critical to our faith and accomplish Your will here through our prayers and our actions—both in public arenas and voting booths. Where the enemy comes to divide and distract us, let the Church arise and pray. Help us resist a spirit of division, and help us love one another as Your children. God, forgive me, and forgive those in Christian churches as a whole, for not interceding more fervently for our nation. May the Holy Spirit direct our pastors to make time to lead our congregations in prayer for our beloved country. Father, may Your Kingdom blessings bring peace and healing to _____ [name of country], Amen.

Let God arise, let His enemies be scattered; let those also who hate Him flee before Him. As smoke is driven away, so drive them away. . . . But let the righteous be glad; let them rejoice before God; yes, let them rejoice exceedingly.

Psalm 68:1–3 nkjv

[Jesus said,] "My house will be called a house of prayer for all nations."

Mark 11:17

FOR MY NEIGHBORHOOD

Lord, I pray that those in my neighborhood will experience Your love. Strengthen the hedge of protection around us, and station Your angels to guard it. I say *no* to the enemy's efforts to cause strife and distrust among families living here. Touch those who need healing—some from disease, others from grief and broken relationships. I pray my neighbors will have strong marriages, family unity, security and a strong faith in You. Be with the parents of young school children in our neighborhood; these parents need Your wisdom and guidance. For those suffering financial lack, show them the way to financial freedom. Lord, help me be a good neighbor, sensitive to encourage or help when needed, but not judging or interfering where I have no business. Lord, bless my neighbors and let Your Kingdom come to this area, Amen.

Do not pervert justice; do not show partiality to the poor or favoritism to the great, but judge your neighbor fairly.

Do not go about spreading slander among your people.

Do not do anything that endangers your neighbor's life. I am the LORD.

LEVITICUS 19:15–16

"The most important one," answered Jesus, "is this: 'Hear, O Israel: the Lord our God, the Lord is one. Love the Lord your God with all your heart and with all your soul and with all your mind and with all your strength.' The second is this: 'Love your neighbor as yourself.' There is no commandment greater than these."

MARK 12:29–31

FOR OUR SCHOOLS

Lord, give wisdom to all those in authority over our children while they're at school. May their schools be a place where unbiased curriculum is taught that does not rewrite history. Bless the teachers with wisdom, compassion and good health. Help school boards and legislators develop school policies that are based on family-friendly values. Father, please intervene and protect our children from the evils of random shootings, gang violence, bullying, drug abuse and promiscuity. May those who plan harm be exposed and dealt with quickly. Cause the devil's strategies against our children to be thwarted, in Jesus' name. Make our schools protected places where students can learn the truth and are encouraged to be good citizens. Let there be in our schools a spiritual awakening that will strengthen Christian youth to share their faith boldly with their peers. Thank You, Lord, for pouring Your grace and favor into our children's lives, Amen.

For the LORD gives wisdom; and from his mouth come knowledge and understanding. He holds success in store for the upright, he is a shield to those whose walk is blameless, for he guards the course of the just and protects the way of his faithful ones.

PROVERBS 2:6–8

Never let loyalty and kindness leave you! Tie them around your neck as a reminder. Write them deep within your heart. Then you will find favor with both God and people, and you will earn a good reputation.

Trust in the LORD with all your heart; do not depend on your own understanding. Seek his will in all you do, and he will show you which path to take.

PROVERBS 3:3–6 NLT

PRAYER FOR MY COMMUNITY

Lord, thank You for the community where I now live—the area where You have led us to establish our home. Help me be a good citizen by voting for officials with sound principles, and by finding ways to volunteer with my talents. May those who don't know You come to a knowledge of Jesus Christ. Help me remain alert to pray for _____ [name of city or community] as You reveal to me both its good and bad points. I pray for peace in this area, where homes, businesses, public buildings and streets will be safe. I stand against the enemy's tactics to promote corruption, drugs, immorality, gangs, thievery, terrorism, greed, deception or false religions. Let evil be exposed and its perpetrators be brought to justice so that goodwill can reign instead. God, pour out Your blessing on our community and let it become what You intend for it to be, Amen.

*This is what the L*ORD *Almighty, the God of Israel, says to all those I carried into exile from Jerusalem to Babylon: " . . . seek the peace and prosperity of the city to which I have carried you into exile. Pray to the L*ORD *for it, because if it prospers, you too will prosper."*

JEREMIAH 29:4, 7

Through the blessing of the upright a city is exalted, but by the mouth of the wicked it is destroyed.

PROVERBS 11:11

PRAYER FOR THE UNBORN

Father, because each of us is fearfully and wonderfully made in Your image, help us protect all infants—preborn and newborn—and give them the right to live. Please show women seeking an abortion how truly precious life is. Thank You for technology that now reveals so much more about human development from the time of conception. Help elected officials grasp a clearer understanding of the sanctity of life and change any of our existing laws that do not uphold it. I pray that women who desire an abortion will choose instead to give birth and allow adoptive parents to provide loving homes for their babies. Lord, help them find the support they need to do this. Grant Your forgiveness to those who are truly sorry for having had an abortion. O God, have mercy and forgive our nation for this sin. May _____ [name of country] become a safe place for the unborn, in Jesus' name, Amen.

Then God said, "And now we will make human beings; they will be like us and resemble us. They will have power over the fish, the birds, and all animals, domestic and wild, large and small." So God created human beings, making them to be like himself. He created them male and female.

GENESIS 1:26–27 GNT

You even formed every bone in my body when you created me in the secret place, carefully, skillfully shaping me from nothing to something. You saw who you created me to be before I became me! Before I'd ever seen the light of day, the number of days you planned for me were already recorded in your book.

PSALM 139:15–16 TPT

FOR REGIONAL DISASTERS

Father, our region has been devastated by the recent _____ [fire, flood, hurricane, tornado, earthquake, etc.], and we need Your miracles. For those whose loved ones are missing, send comfort and hope for rescue. For those whose property has suffered damage and loss, let them know they're not forsaken or abandoned. I pray that government and insurance agencies, as well as charitable organizations, will respond quickly to the challenge of restoring the losses. Lord, give hope to those who are grieving. Help them recover, both emotionally and economically. Bless the many volunteers sacrificing their time and energy to help to save lives, livestock and buildings. Keep away looters who take advantage of others' losses, and scammers who overcharge for clearing land and rebuilding structures. Thank You in advance for giving wisdom and comfort to all of us affected by this disaster. Nothing is impossible for You, Almighty God, Amen.

God is our refuge and strength, an ever-present help in trouble. Therefore we will not fear, though the earth give way and the mountains fall into the heart of the sea, though its waters roar and foam and the mountains quake with their surging. . . .

*The L*ORD *Almighty is with us; the God of Jacob is our fortress.*

PSALM 46:1–3, 11

All praise to God, the Father of our Lord Jesus Christ. God is our merciful Father and the source of all comfort. He comforts us in all our troubles so that we can comfort others. When they are troubled, we will be able to give them the same comfort God has given us.

2 CORINTHIANS 1:3–4 NLT

FOR OUR NATION'S DEFENDERS

*L*ord, grant Your protection and blessing over all who wear the uniform to protect our nation or aid those in crisis: members of all branches of our military at home and abroad, law enforcement personnel, border patrol officers, fire fighters, park rangers, emergency medical technicians and other first responders who put themselves in harm's way for our safety. Lord, give them courage and wise judgment as they enforce our laws, and as they respond at the risk of their lives to shootings, terrorist attacks, fires and other disasters. May their families know Your peace, strength and comfort while their loved ones are on the job. For those who have experienced traumatic injuries that are still troubling them, please heal their bodies, minds and emotions. Lord, send messengers to share the truth of Your love and grace with those who don't know You. Thank You for all the brave ones who work hard to keep us safe, Amen.

Come to me, all you who are weary and burdened, and I will give you rest. Take my yoke upon you and learn from me, for I am gentle and humble in heart, and you will find rest for your souls. For my yoke is easy and my burden is light.

MATTHEW 11:28–30

God is not unjust; he will not forget your work and the love you have shown him as you have helped his people and continue to help them.

HEBREWS 6:10

LORD, PROTECT OUR NATION

Heavenly Father, please protect our nation from those who seek to cause harm and instill fear in the hearts of the people. Guard our ports and borders, our government buildings, military bases, all educational facilities, places of worship, public buildings, stadiums, financial institutions, the postal system, bridges, ship channels, water conduits and all transportation systems. Protect our electrical and nuclear energy plants, gas/oil distribution centers, hospital and medical facilities, space centers and research facilities, law enforcement agencies, farmlands and residential communities. Defend us against the spread of infectious diseases, germ warfare or cyber attacks. Protect and grant wisdom to those who are charged with enforcing the law and maintaining order in all these venues. Lord, may the prayers of Your people help establish a shield over _____ [name of nation] that the enemy cannot penetrate. I give You great praise for answering this prayer, in Jesus' name, Amen.

The Lord gives victory to his anointed. He answers him from his heavenly sanctuary with the victorious power of his right hand. Some trust in chariots and some in horses, but we trust in the name of the Lord our God. They are brought to their knees and fall, but we rise up and stand firm.

Psalm 20:6–8

May there be no enemy breaking through our walls, no going into captivity, no cries of alarm in our town squares. Yes, joyful are those who live like this! Joyful indeed are those whose God is the Lord.

Psalm 144:14–15 nlt

FOR MY STATE

(Note that from this point on, the rest of part 9's prayers are written with the United States in mind, but you can substitute wording that would make each prayer applicable to your own country.)

Lord, thank You for the uniqueness, beauty and natural resources of my state. I pray that voters will elect God-minded men and women to serve as our governor, legislators and judges. Give our public servants wisdom to establish policies that benefit all our citizens. I stand against the efforts of the enemy to turn our state into a stronghold that compromises religious, political and civil liberties. Bless and prosper our residents who work in private and public businesses, government offices, factories, educational facilities, health care services, housing, the food industry, agriculture, transportation, tourism and law enforcement. Let there be new discoveries that provide more jobs and draw industries to our state. Father, may we experience an economic boom and see poverty eliminated. Let hate crimes be stopped before they occur. Grant us peace, prosperity and a spiritual awakening that will cause many people to receive Your love. Thank You for these blessings, Amen.

You, Lord, will keep the needy safe and will protect us forever from the wicked, who freely strut about when what is vile is honored by the human race.

Psalm 12:7–8

This is what the Lord says. . . .

It is I who made the earth and created mankind on it. My own hands stretched out the heavens; I marshaled their starry hosts.

Isaiah 45:11–12

PRAYER FOR ELECTIONS

Father, I pray for moral, honest men and women to find support and be elected in local, state and national elections. I ask You to expose corruption, covert agendas, immorality and special interests. May hidden things be brought to light and dealt with speedily. Cause any elected officials with evil intentions to be replaced by candidates with integrity and a heart to honor our laws and constitution. Lord, send angelic forces to dismantle any plans of the enemy in which he seeks to manipulate our election process—the essential foundation of our freedoms. I pray there will be no corruption or vote stealing. Help our citizens be informed, responsible voters. May they be diligent to go to the polls and use godly values as their standard when they cast their ballots. Thank You, Lord, for the freedom we enjoy to elect those who govern our nation, Amen.

I will always obey your law, for ever and ever. I will walk about in freedom, for I have sought out your precepts. I will speak of your statutes before kings and will not be put to shame.

PSALM 119:44–46

I urge, then, first of all, that petitions, prayers, intercession and thanksgiving be made for all people— for kings and all those in authority, that we may live peaceful and quiet lives in all godliness and holiness.

1 TIMOTHY 2:1–2

PRAYER FOR OUR PRESIDENT

Father, in obedience to Your Word, I pray today for President _____ [name], the leader of our nation and of the free world. Because this office comes with such grave responsibility, I pray that he will call on You to give him the wisdom and endurance he needs to fulfill this office. May the evil strategies plotted against him come to nothing, and may those trying to harm our country be stopped, in Jesus' name. Surround our president with advisors who will offer sound counsel regarding crucial decisions he faces daily. Overshadow our president and his family with good health and divine protection, and also the vice-president and his family, the cabinet and all the advisors. Lord, please assign angels to watch over them, and raise up an army of believers who will pray for them faithfully. As I bring this request to You, I give thanks for the freedom of religion we enjoy in America, Amen.

For we do not have a High Priest who cannot sympathize with our weaknesses, but was in all points tempted as we are, yet without sin. Let us therefore come boldly to the throne of grace, that we may obtain mercy and find grace to help in time of need.

Hebrews 4:15–16 NKJV

Pray for every political leader and representative, so that we would be able to live tranquil, undisturbed lives, as we worship the awe-inspiring God with pure hearts. It is pleasing to our Savior-God to pray for them.

1 Timothy 2:2–3 TPT

WISDOM FOR GOVERNMENT LEADERS

*L*ord, I ask forgiveness for the sins of America and for the opposition against acknowledging You in our government agencies. Impart godly wisdom to the president, vice-president, cabinet, members of Congress (both House and Senate) and those in the judicial branch. May truth, discernment and discretion guide their decisions both in their public and private lives, especially when they're creating laws that govern our country. Please show them that being in a position of power to represent the well-being of their constituents is a sacred trust. I also pray that our leaders will take action to improve immigration laws and do whatever is necessary to protect our borders against criminals and harmful elements. Thank You that our Founders honored You by establishing our constitutional republic on prayer and the Scriptures. May that foundation be reinforced, and may the rule of law be paramount and respected by all those in authority, in Jesus' name, Amen.

If my people, who are called by my name, will humble themselves and pray and seek my face and turn from their wicked ways, then I will hear from heaven, and I will forgive their sin and will heal their land.

2 Chronicles 7:14

If any of you lacks wisdom, you should ask God, who gives generously to all without finding fault, and it will be given to you. But when you ask, you must believe and not doubt, because the one who doubts is like a wave of the sea, blown and tossed by the wind.

James 1:5–6

FOR THE JUDICIAL SYSTEM

Thank You, Lord, that our Founders established three branches of government to ensure that there would be a balance of powers. Forgive us for drifting so far from this principle. Please remove those judges who ignore constitutional rights and legislate from the bench. Make a way for honorable judges who will correctly interpret the law to replace them. Grant wisdom to our Supreme Court justices and to the thousands of judges serving across America in federal, state, county and municipal courts. May they not be swayed by prejudice, political opinion or malicious outside influences. Lord, as our courts come into alignment with Your will, also cause needed changes to be established in all levels of our correctional system. Thank You for awakening believers to pray for these reforms to happen, and to vote accordingly. May all forces of evil in our judicial and correctional systems be abolished, in Jesus' name, Amen.

He has shown you, O man, what is good; and what does the LORD require of you but to do justly, to love mercy, and to walk humbly with your God?

MICAH 6:8 NKJV

He [Jehoshaphat] appointed judges in the land. . . . He told them, "Consider carefully what you do, because you are not judging for mere mortals but for the LORD, who is with you whenever you give a verdict. Now let the fear of the LORD be on you. Judge carefully, for with the LORD our God there is no injustice or partiality or bribery."

2 CHRONICLES 19:5–7

PRAYER FOR THE MEDIA

*F*ather, thank You that in America we have freedom of the press without government control. Thank You for those who have fought to defend this right. But now, with many more print, Internet and broadcast outlets, truthful reporting is under serious attack. The enemy is using some channels and reporters to promote false news that deceives many people. Correspondents can sway voters' opinions by reporting purposely slanted news. Lord, expose and remove those with evil agendas. Grant favor to journalists, editors and producers who are diligent in reporting the news without bias. Empower them with wisdom and courage. Bless and protect them, so the public receives a truthful narrative of news and events. And please, Lord, raise up more people in the media who will operate with integrity and godly principles. Thank You, Amen.

Many will follow their depraved conduct and will bring the way of truth into disrepute. In their greed these teachers will exploit you with fabricated stories.

2 PETER 2:2–3

But if you harbor bitter envy and selfish ambition in your hearts, do not boast about it or deny the truth. Such "wisdom" does not come down from heaven but is earthly, unspiritual, demonic. For where you have envy and selfish ambition, there you find disorder and every evil practice.

. . . Peacemakers who sow in peace reap a harvest of righteousness.

JAMES 3:14–16, 18

FOR THE ENTERTAINMENT INDUSTRY

O God, I'm praying for Your intervention to shift the negative influence much of Hollywood has had over our nation. The enemy uses the entertainment industry to try to corrupt our society, especially our youth, and to distort the difference between right and wrong. Thank You that we are now seeing wholesome, faith-based films appearing in theaters. Strengthen those who have the courage to write such scripts and to produce or play the roles in these movies and documentaries. Please protect them, despite attacks from their peers and the secular media. Provide favor, funding and opportunities for those who seek to produce wholesome forms of entertainment—whether movies, TV programs, Broadway shows, musicals or other avenues. Please give inspired ideas to the writers, producers, directors, actors, editors and film crews as they create new material with a positive impact. Lord, may a paradigm shift in this part of our culture contribute to the spiritual awakening that You have promised to send, Amen.

I have a message from God in my heart concerning the sinfulness of the wicked: There is no fear of God before their eyes.

In their own eyes they flatter themselves too much to detect or hate their sin. The words of their mouths are wicked and deceitful; they fail to act wisely or do good.

Psalm 36:1–3

I will walk within my house with a perfect heart.

I will set nothing wicked before my eyes; I hate the work of those who fall away; it shall not cling to me. A perverse heart shall depart from me; I will not know wickedness.

Psalm 101:2–4 NKJV

Declaration

I declare that I will be a good citizen by voting for officials and representatives in all branches of government who have godly principles. When possible, I will volunteer my services where I am needed. I will pray for peace in my community and the entire nation, and I will stand against the enemy's tactics that promote immorality and violence throughout the land. I decree that hidden things will be revealed, officials with malicious agendas will be removed, and enemy assignments that are aligned against God's purposes for _____ [name of country] will be demolished. I beseech the Lord to give all area and national leaders great wisdom concerning crucial decisions they will be making. I will continue declaring, "May God's Kingdom come and His will be done in my country!" I claim that as God's people are faithful to pray for _____ [name of country], righteousness will exalt our nation [see Proverbs 14:34].

PART 10

IMPORTANT *Prayer* HELPS

A MOST IMPORTANT PRAYER

Jesus Christ, God's Son, came to earth and took the blame for the sin of our pride, rebellion and selfishness that separated all humankind from God. Thus He bridged the gap between us and our Creator, reconciling us to the Father. When we repent and confess our sin, God willingly forgives us and cleanses us from the past so we can freely come to Him with our needs. You can make Jesus the Lord of your life by praying this most important prayer:

Lord Jesus, I confess that I've sinned against You. Please forgive me for walking in my own selfish ways, and wash me clean. I receive You as my Lord and Savior. I believe You are the Son of God who came to earth, died on the cross, shed Your blood for my sins and arose from the dead. Lord, strengthen me to live my life to please You. Thank You for opening the way for me to be saved and to pray directly to God the Father in Your name. I rejoice in Your promise that I will live with You forever in heaven, Amen.

[Be] always thankful to the Father who has made us fit to share all the wonderful things that belong to those who live in the Kingdom of light. For he has rescued us out of the darkness and gloom of Satan's kingdom and brought us into the Kingdom of his dear Son, who bought our freedom with his blood and forgave us all our sins.

COLOSSIANS 1:12–14 TLB

THE LORD'S PRAYER

When Jesus was teaching His disciples and the multitudes on the mountainside, He gave them a simple model for prayer that is known today as "the Lord's Prayer" or "the Our Father." He told them,

Your Father knows the things you have need of before you ask Him. In this manner, therefore, pray:

Our Father in heaven,
Hallowed be Your name.
Your kingdom come.
Your will be done
On earth as it is in heaven.
Give us this day our daily bread.
And forgive us our debts,
As we forgive our debtors.
And do not lead us into temptation,
But deliver us from the evil one.
For Yours is the kingdom and the power
*   and the glory forever.*
Amen.

MATTHEW 6:8–13 NKJV

WORSHIP STARTERS

*P*raise is a good way to begin any prayer time. Try entering into worship and prayer by using the letters of the alphabet. Focus on the attributes of the Trinity—our heavenly Father's goodness, Jesus' sacrifice and the Holy Spirit as our Comforter. Here is a starter list[1] you can add to:

A: Abba Father, Almighty God, Ancient of Days
B: Bread of Life, Blood of the Lamb, Breath of Life
C: Creator, Counselor, Covenant Keeper
D: Deliverer, Destroyer of sin
E: Eternal, Everlasting God
F: Father, Faithful Friend
G: Giver of life, Gracious One

1. This list is adapted from Quin Sherrer, *A Mother's Guide to Praying for Your Children* (Chosen, 2011), 135–37.

H: Healer, Helper
I: I AM, Immanuel, Immortal
J: Jehovah, Just Judge
K: King of kings, Keeper
L: Lord of lords, Lamb of God, Living Water
M: Messiah, Master, Merciful Lord
N: Name above all names, Nazarene
O: Omnipotent, Omniscient, Omega
P: Prince of Peace, Protector, Provider
Q: Quieter of my storms
R: Redeemer, Righteous One, Rescuer
S: Savior, Son of God, Shepherd
T: Teacher, Truth, Triumphant
U: Universal, Upright, Unchangeable
V: Victorious, Vine, Voice of God
W: Warrior, the Word, Way Maker
X: Extraordinary in all Your ways
Y: Yahweh (*YHWH*—Hebrew name of God, Jehovah)
Z: Zealous—"He will arouse His zeal like a man of war" (Isaiah 42:13 NASB)

PART 11
Scriptures for INTERCESSION & WARFARE

UNDERSTANDING THE ENEMY

*Now the serpent was more crafty than any of the wild animals the L*ORD *God had made. He said to the woman, "Did God really say, 'You must not eat from any tree in the garden'?" . . .*

*Then the L*ORD *God said to the woman, "What is this you have done?"*

The woman said, "The serpent deceived me, and I ate."

GENESIS 3:1, 13

How you are fallen from heaven, O Lucifer, son of the morning! . . . For you have said in your heart: "I will ascend into heaven, I will exalt my throne above the stars of God; . . . I will be like the Most

High." Yet you shall be brought down to Sheol, to the lowest depths of the Pit.

Isaiah 14:12–15 NKJV

Do not be afraid of them [our enemies]; remember the Lord who is great and awesome, and fight for your brothers, your sons, your daughters, your wives and your houses.

Nehemiah 4:14 NASB

You are unable to hear what I [Jesus] say. You belong to your father, the devil, and you want to carry out your father's desires. He was a murderer from the beginning, not holding to the truth, for there is no truth in him. When he lies, he speaks his native language, for he is a liar and the father of lies.

John 8:43–44

The god of this age has blinded the minds of unbelievers, so that they cannot see the light of the gospel that displays the glory of Christ, who is the image of God.

2 Corinthians 4:4

"In your anger do not sin": Do not let the sun go down while you are still angry, and do not give the devil a foothold. . . .

. . . Get rid of all bitterness, rage and anger, brawling and slander, along with every form of malice.

Ephesians 4:26–27, 31

Put on the full armor of God, so that you can take your stand against the devil's schemes. For our struggle is not against flesh and blood, but against the rulers, against the authorities, against the powers of this dark world and against the spiritual forces of evil in the heavenly realms.

Ephesians 6:11–12

Submit therefore to God. Resist the devil and he will flee from you. Draw near to God and He will draw near to you. . . . Humble yourselves in the presence of the Lord, and He will exalt you.

JAMES 4:7–8, 10 NASB

Then I heard a loud voice in heaven saying, "Now God's salvation has come! Now God has shown his power as King! Now his Messiah has shown his authority! For the one who stood before our God and accused believers day and night has been thrown out of heaven."

REVELATION 12:10 GNT

GOD'S ANSWERS AND PROMISES

Moses told the people, "Don't be afraid. Just stand still and watch the Lord rescue you today. The Egyptians you see today will never be seen again. The Lord himself will fight for you. Just stay calm."

EXODUS 14:13–14 NLT

The eternal God is your refuge, and underneath are the everlasting arms. He will drive out your enemies before you, saying, "Destroy them!"

DEUTERONOMY 33:27

For the eyes of the Lord range throughout the earth to strengthen those whose hearts are fully committed to him.

2 CHRONICLES 16:9

Give us aid against the enemy, for human help is worthless. With God we will gain the victory, and he will trample down our enemies.

Psalm 108:12–13

So shall My word be that goes forth from My mouth; it shall not return to Me void, but it shall accomplish what I please, and it shall prosper in the thing for which I sent it.

Isaiah 55:11 NKJV

Jesus replied, ". . . I watched Satan topple until he fell suddenly from heaven like lightning to the ground. Now you understand that I have imparted to you all my authority to trample over his kingdom. You will trample upon every demon before you and overcome every power Satan possesses. Absolutely nothing will be able to harm you as you walk in this authority."

Luke 10:18–19 TPT

For God so loved the world that he gave his one and only Son, that whoever believes in him shall not perish but have eternal life. For God did not send his Son into the world to condemn the world, but to save the world through him.

John 3:16–17

I [Jesus] do not pray that You should take them out of the world, but that You should keep them from the evil one.

John 17:15 nkjv

I [Jesus] am sending you [Paul] to them [the Gentiles] to open their eyes and turn them from darkness to light, and from the power of Satan to God, so that they may receive forgiveness of sins.

Acts 26:17–18

For I am persuaded that neither death nor life, nor angels nor principalities nor powers, nor things present nor things to come, nor height nor depth, nor any other created thing, shall be able to separate us from the love of God which is in Christ Jesus our Lord.

Romans 8:38–39 nkjv

The weapons we fight with are not the weapons of the world. On the contrary, they have divine power to demolish strongholds. We demolish arguments and every pretension that sets itself up against the knowledge of God, and we take captive every thought to make it obedient to Christ.

2 Corinthians 10:4–5

God exalted him to the highest place and gave him the name that is above every name, that at the name of Jesus every knee should bow, in heaven and on earth and under the earth, and every tongue acknowledge that Jesus Christ is Lord, to the glory of God the Father.

Philippians 2:9–11

He [God] forgave all our sins. He canceled the record of the charges against us and took it away by nailing it to the cross. In this way, he disarmed the spiritual rulers and authorities. He shamed them publicly by his victory over them on the cross.

Colossians 2:13–15 nlt

For the word of God is living and active, sharper than any two-edged sword, piercing to the division of soul and of spirit, of joints and of marrow, and discerning the thoughts and intentions of the heart.

Hebrews 4:12 esv

Let us throw off everything that hinders and the sin that so easily entangles. And let us run with perseverance the race marked out for us, fixing our eyes on Jesus.

Hebrews 12:1–2

The Lord is not slow in keeping his promise, as some understand slowness. Instead he is patient with you, not wanting anyone to perish, but everyone to come to repentance.

2 Peter 3:9

They triumphed over him [our accuser] by the blood of the Lamb and by the word of their testimony.

Revelation 12:11

Continued from page 4.

Unless otherwise indicated, Scripture quotations are from the Holy Bible, New International Version®. NIV®. Copyright © 1973, 1978, 1984, 2011 by Biblica, Inc.™ Used by permission of Zondervan. All rights reserved worldwide. www.zondervan.com. The "NIV" and "New International Version" are trademarks registered in the United States Patent and Trademark Office by Biblica, Inc.™

Scripture quotations identified AMP are from the Amplified® Bible (AMP), copyright © 2015 by The Lockman Foundation. Used by permission. www.Lockman.org

Scripture quotations identified AMPC are from the Amplified® Bible (AMPC), copyright © 1954, 1958, 1962, 1964, 1965, 1987 by The Lockman Foundation. Used by permission. www.Lockman.org

Scripture quotations identified ESV are from The Holy Bible, English Standard Version® (ESV®), copyright © 2001 by Crossway, a publishing ministry of Good News Publishers. Used by permission. All rights reserved. ESV Text Edition: 2016

Scripture quotations identified GNT are from the Good News Translation in Today's English Version-Second Edition. Copyright © 1992 by American Bible Society. Used by permission.

Scripture quotations identified ISV taken from the Holy Bible: International Standard Version®. Copyright © 1996-forever by The ISV Foundation. ALL RIGHTS RESERVED INTERNATIONALLY. Used by permission.

Scripture quotations identified MEV taken from the Modern English Version. Copyright © 2014 by Military Bible Association. Used by permission. All rights reserved.

Scripture quotations identified NASB are from the New American Standard Bible® (NASB), copyright © 1960, 1962, 1963, 1968, 1971, 1972, 1973, 1975, 1977, 1995 by The Lockman Foundation. Used by permission. www.Lockman.org

Scripture quotations identified NKJV are from the New King James Version®. Copyright © 1982 by Thomas Nelson. Used by permission. All rights reserved.

Scripture quotations identified NLT are from the *Holy Bible*, New Living Translation, copyright © 1996, 2004, 2007, 2013, 2015 by Tyndale House Foundation. Used by permission of Tyndale House Publishers, Inc., Carol Stream, Illinois 60188. All rights reserved.

Scripture quotations identified TLB are from The Living Bible, copyright © 1971. Used by permission of Tyndale House Publishers, Inc., Carol Stream, Illinois 60188. All rights reserved.

Scripture quotations identified TPT are from The Passion Translation®. Copyright © 2017, 2018 by Passion & Fire Ministries, Inc. Used by permission. All rights reserved. ThePassionTranslation.com.

Scripture quotations identified VOICE taken from The Voice™. Copyright © 2012 by Ecclesia Bible Society. Used by permission. All rights reserved.

Quin Sherrer has written or co-authored 31 books, primarily with Ruthanne Garlock, including bestsellers *A Woman's Guide to Spiritual Warfare* and *How to Pray for Your Children*. Their book *God Be with Us* was a finalist in the devotional class for Gold Medallion awards, given in recognition of excellence in Christian literature by the Evangelical Christian Publishers Association.

Quin has spoken to audiences in 47 states and 12 nations, and has been a guest on more than 370 radio and television programs. She holds a B.S. degree in journalism from Florida State University. For some years she wrote for newspapers and magazines in the Cape Kennedy, Florida, area, where her late husband, LeRoy, was a NASA aerospace engineer. A winner of *Guideposts* magazine's writing contest, she also was named Writer of the Year at the Florida Writers in Touch Conference.

Quin previously served on the Aglow International board of directors. She often speaks on her book topics at Christian retreats and seminars. You can contact her at www.quinsherrer.com.

Ruthanne Garlock is a Bible teacher and author with a varied background in international ministry to 35 nations. She has co-authored 20 books on prayer and related subjects with Quin Sherrer, plus writing two missions biographies on her own.

Ruthanne and her late husband, John, served with Continental Theological Seminary in Brussels, Belgium, for four years. They then served at Christ For The Nations (CFN) in Dallas, Texas, where John was an instructor and Ruthanne worked as a freelance writer and teacher. In 2018, CFN presented her with the prestigious Freda Lindsay Award.

Ruthanne holds a B.A. degree in Bible and theology from Central Bible College, Springfield, Missouri, and is ordained with World Ministry Fellowship, Plano, Texas. Now living in the Texas hill country, Ruthanne continues the work of Garlock Ministries through her teaching and writing, and through raising funds to help provide education for more than 100 orphans in a remote province of Zimbabwe. You can contact her at www.garlockministries.org.